SCHOLASTIC

GRAMMAR
PUNCTUATION & SPELLING
SATs CHALLENGE
Year 6

Teacher's Guide

Scholastic Education, an imprint of Scholastic Ltd

Book End, Range Road, Witney, Oxfordshire, OX29 0YD

Registered office: Westfield Road, Southam, Warwickshire CV47 0RA

www.scholastic.co.uk

1 2 3 4 5 6 7 8 9   8 9 0 1 2 3 4 5 6 7

British Library Cataloguing-in-Publication Data

A catalogue record for this book is available from the British Library.

ISBN 978-1407-17650-5

Printed and bound by Ashford Colour Press

Author Shelley Welsh

Editorial Rachel Morgan, Shannon Keenlyside, Audrey Stokes, Margaret Eaton, Mo Dutton, Julia Roberts

Cover and Series Design Neil Salt, Nicolle Thomas and Alice Duggan

Layout Alice Duggan

Illustrations Robin Lawrie/Beehive illustration

Contents

About the book

This book is part of the *Scholastic SATs Challenge Programme*. It is designed to be used in conjunction with the *Skills Tests Papers* and *Workbook*.

The introduction provides overview information about how to support and challenge children in your school. This book has been written with different units which are numbered for ease-of-reference, but it is designed to work flexibly for your needs and does not need to be covered sequentially (see page 5 for more information). There are also a number of photocopiable resource sheets provided including an attendance chart, reward certificate and a letter for parents. A curriculum coverage overview to allow you to locate specific needs easily is also provided.

Each unit follows the same structure. It is intended each session will take around 20 minutes and each unit could form multiple sessions, if required.

- **Objectives:** the objectives that the unit covers are provided.

- **What the children need to know:** a brief summary of the key points that the children need to know about the focus of the unit.

- **Test links:** test and question references to help you find related questions in the *Skills Test Papers* quickly.

- **Workbook links:** page references to the *Workbook* which relate to all or part of the unit.

- **Mastery and challenge ideas:** a range of challenging different ideas have been provided for each unit. It is not intended that all of these would be completed in a single session (or that all would need to be completed), rather that you would choose the most appropriate tasks for your children's needs.

- **Review:** suggestions on how to review and assess learning, including lines of questioning, example questions and short activities.

- **Watch and listen:** examples of learning to look and watch for that may indicate mastery and depth of understanding of the topic

At the end of the book are a range of photocopiable pages. These pages are generally linked to specific units and activities. However, there are also a group of photocopiable pages which provide writing topics to allow practice and use grammar, spelling and punctuation in real-life contexts.

How to use *Challenge* in the classroom

Challenge has been designed to be used with children who are working at the expected standard and above. It is a mastery series which will work alongside your general class teaching.

All materials have been designed so they are initially accessible to most children but provide opportunity for stretch to those looking for and able to take on more of a challenge. It provides the flexibility to be used in a variety ways so you can choose which works best for you and your children.

As a **dip in/dip out whole-class resource** it can be used at any point during the year and leading up to the National Tests. Most units in the *Teacher's Guide* have a topic focus which reflects National Curriculum objectives rather than specific test practice which makes them perfect to use through the year. Target the topics which need the most focused practice or choose a topic and corresponding tests to provide additional challenge or deepen understanding.

You may also want to use the series to provide **small-group practice** for children working above expected standard or children who are working at expected standard but would benefit from additional challenge. Use it to provide challenging tasks and practice at any time throughout the year or as part of your SATs preparation. The topic focus allows for grouping children by their areas of weakness or strength and target these specifically. This could mean that different groups of children are working on different topics at the same time. If you are using additional classes outside of school hours then you will need to ask parental permission; a letter template has been provided for this on page 15.

In a run-up to SATs it could also be used as a **twice-weekly programme** used 8–12 weeks in advance of the National Tests. Start by giving children the first all-topic test and spelling test as an initial assessment. Work through the units consecutively or focus on those topics which the all-topic test highlighted as an area in need of additional practice. Next, practice and assess by topic using the topic assessment tests. Complete the second all-topic test and spelling test for further SATs-style practice and assess progress.

Whichever way you use the programme, use can use the *Teacher's Guide* for classroom ideas and support this with the activities in the *Workbook*. The *Skills Test Papers* can be used to identify areas to focus upon and to practise and consolidate learning.

Supporting and challenging more confident learners

All children need to be challenged and supported in their learning. For more confident learners, how is this best done? Will it look significantly different from other groups of learners?

With a mastery approach to learning, it should not be significantly different from one group of learners to another. With this in mind, do not limit these strategies to confident learners but make them available to all children, where appropriate.

Encourage a positive mindset

Foster a positive mindset among all children. It is not only children who are struggling who need to move away from a fixed mindset, in thinking they are not 'clever'. Children who see themselves as 'clever' may often resist engaging in tasks that are more challenging or where they think they may fail for fear of making mistakes, which would make them look and feel 'less clever'. This type of fixed mindset will limit children's progress even if they are performing above expected levels. Tackle this by:

- Explaining to children that it is through mistakes that we learn and encouraging them to take risks in their learning, such as aiming to write sentences that are more structurally challenging and to include more complicated vocabulary even if they are unsure of how to spell certain words.

- Fostering an environment where mistakes are not only accepted but celebrated. Obviously, in a test setting this is not realistic but leading up to the National Tests and practising for them need not emphasise success based on a score. Praise sharing of errors and focus on the effort made and risk taken rather than having the correct answer. Ask who got a *different* answer rather than asking who got that *right*. Share work with 'interesting' errors with the class and encourage children to do the same. Work through problems together.

Learn deeply rather than move on to 'harder' material

Allow time to look at topics in depth, keeping children's interest by providing them with a wide range of tasks rather than giving them 'more of the same, but harder'. This *Teacher's Guide* provides you with a variety of ideas and activities to choose from to keep children challenged and interested. Look for ways to extend and enhance both these and your own favourite activities. Many of the activity ideas and 'Watch and listen' points will offer suggestions on how to take a topic or activity further. Consider whether children could explore a topic more on their own such as an investigation of English words with Germanic origins in the context of tricky spellings. You may also wish to use the *Workbook* to provide additional practice which children could move on to independently once they have completed an activity.

Apply learning to real-life experiences

Being able to apply what they have learned in both familiar and new situations will stretch and motivate children. Real-life contexts will provide greater meaning to many topics, particularly subjects such as grammar which may seem disconnected from everyday life. Writing tasks which require children to use grammar, punctuation and vocabulary they have learned will embed the learning and lead to deeper understanding. Look for opportunities around the home and school, such as writing a letter to the local council arguing for a zebra crossing outside the school. Ask children to carefully consider how they might use modal verbs to make their argument effectively.

Encourage reflection and exploration through discussion

Most National Test questions will not ask children to explain their thinking but being able to do this will deepen their understanding and bring to light any areas of misconception which can quickly be addressed; both of which will have an overall positive impact on their learning as well as test results. More confident learners may be able to answer a question quickly but this will not necessarily be an indicator of depth of knowledge. Expect children to dig deeper by encouraging them to explain not only *what* they know but *how* they know it. Use a variety of open-ended questions to get children talking.

Provide opportunities for children to reflect, explore and discuss what they know across subjects and throughout the day. Below are a few strategies and examples for getting children reasoning and talking about grammar, punctuation and spelling.

- Ask children to tell you what is the same or different about these two sentences.

  I know you would have helped your brother with his homework.

  I know you could have helped your brother with his homework.

Children would notice that both sentences are in the conditional and that all the words are the same, apart from the modal verbs, *could* and *would*. Ideally, they would discuss how this difference subtly changes the meaning of each sentence.

- Make a statement and then ask children to consider, based on this statement and their knowledge of the wider topic, what else do we know?

  To have + a present participle is how we form a verb in the present perfect. For example, I have bought her a gift for her birthday.

Children might talk about how *to be* will change based on the subject and that the present participle would stay the same. They may bring up the past perfect and how it is formed in the same way or discuss actions in the past in broader terms.

- Make a statement and ask children to consider if it is sometimes, always or never true. Ask them to provide examples to support their thinking.

  A sentence has a subject.

If a child answered *never* then you could assume they do not understand what a subject is. An answer of *sometimes* may lead to a discussion of imperative sentences and how the subject is the listener.

- Choose a topic and ask children to give you a peculiar and obvious example. They should be able to explain their choices.

  Think about prefixes and give me a peculiar and obvious example.

If a child's examples were *unneat* and *undone* they might explain that *unnneat* is peculiar because it is rarely used and offer an explanation of why. For example, it looks strange when written and is also awkward to say.

Achieving and identifying mastery

In simple terms, **mastery** can be defined as: *comprehensive knowledge or skill in a particular subject or activity.*

It follows that a child with a higher level of mastery will not only have a deep understanding of a subject but score higher in the National Tests than a child with a lower level, even if they know the same content.

With this is in mind, how can you achieve and identify mastery with greater depth with the *SATs Challenge* programme?

Achieving mastery

The mastery and challenge activities in this *Teacher's Guide* offer a variety of engaging activities to choose from. Aim to include a range of activities to develop children's fluency, reasoning and problem-solving skills. Photocopiable materials support and extend these activities. The *Workbook* gives children further practice in each topic and allows them to consolidate their learning and deepen their understanding.

For each subject, how to ensure mastery will require slightly different strategies which are outlined in the *Teacher's Guide*. However, across all subjects: provide opportunities for children to explain their thinking and to use what they have learned previously and to apply in new situations; encourage a steady but deep pace, rather than rushing on to a new topic; apply learning to real-life experiences where possible, and show its purpose; and aim for more 'children's voice' than 'teacher's voice', encouraging them to explain their thinking and explore topics thoroughly.

Identifying mastery

What will mastery at greater depth look like?

For example, if the objective is to learn the function of sentences, children demonstrating mastery may experiment in turning questions into statements:

Are you going to badminton this evening? ⟶ *You are going to badminton this evening.*

They will recognise that a command sentence does not necessarily start with the command verb and experiment accordingly:

After you have brushed your teeth, put your shoes on.

How do I identify it?

The tests in the *Skills Test Papers* can be used not only to quickly assess children's understanding of a topic before or after reviewing but, by looking at specific questions in depth, provide an excellent starting point for an assessment of depth of mastery of a topic or objective. For example, for the following test question you might ask questions such as: *Can you think of another adverbial to replace 'after' which has a similar meaning? What about one that would change the meaning? How and why does the punctuation change when you rewrite the sentence? Why might you choose to start your sentence with an adverbial rather than put it at the end?*

I. Rewrite the sentence below so that it starts with the **adverbial**.

Luke and Heba were exhausted after their long hike up the mountain.

_____

Each unit in this _Teacher's Guide_ has a series of 'Watch and listen' points which describe what mastery at greater depth might look like in relation to the topic covered. Keep these points in mind when working through activities, as well as when children are working independently in the _Workbook_. Ask them to explain their thinking as they work and extend practice questions with further questioning.

Working at greater depth

Below are two tables that list the National Curriculum objectives for grammar, vocabulary and punctuation, and spelling. The objectives have been broken down to indicate what children should be demonstrating if they are working at greater depth in these areas. Use this list as another tool to help you track and assess children's mastery of a topic and depth of understanding.

Grammar, vocabulary and punctuation

National Curriculum objective	Working at greater depth
Recognise vocabulary and structures that are appropriate for formal speech and writing, including subjunctive forms.	Can manage shifts between levels of formality through selecting vocabulary precisely and by manipulating grammatical structures.
Use passive verbs to affect the presentation of information in a sentence.	Can select verb forms for meaning and effect.
Use the perfect form of verbs to mark relationships of time and cause.	Can select verb forms for meaning and effect.
Use expanded noun phrases to convey complicated information concisely.	Can enhance meaning or atmosphere through using expanded noun phrases.
Use modal verbs or adverbs to indicate degrees of possibility.	Can accurately and appropriately use modal verbs or adverbs to indicate degrees of possibility, precisely choosing the effect wanted.
Use relative clauses beginning with _who, which, where, when, whose, that_ or with an implied (omitted) relative pronoun.	Can use relative clauses beginning with _who, which, where, when, whose, that_ or with an implied (omitted) relative pronoun in their own writing to create precision and atmosphere.
Learning the grammar for Year 6 in English Appendix 2.	Can use synonyms and antonyms to create effects in writing. Can use vocabulary to create a sense of formality or informality in writing. Can confidently use subjunctive verbs to create formality.
Use commas to clarify meaning or avoid ambiguity in writing.	Can confidently and independently use commas to clarify meaning or avoid ambiguity correctly in writing.

Achieving and identifying mastery

National Curriculum objective	Working at greater depth
Use hyphens to avoid ambiguity.	Can confidently and independently use hyphens to avoid ambiguity.
Use brackets, dashes or commas to indicate parenthesis.	Can use brackets, dashes or commas to indicate parenthesis, using the most appropriate or showing personal preference.
Use semi-colons, colons or dashes to mark boundaries between independent clauses.	Confidently uses semi-colons, colons or dashes to mark boundaries between independent clauses, choosing the most appropriate or showing personal preference.
Use a colon to introduce a list.	Can correctly and confidently use a colon to introduce a list where appropriate; can correctly punctuate the rest of the sentence.
Punctuate bullet points consistently.	Can punctuate bullet points consistently, choosing punctuation to suit the complexity of the list.
Use and understand the grammatical terminology in English Appendix 2 accurately and appropriately in discussing their writing and reading.	Can use and understand a wide range of grammatical terminology beyond those outlined in Appendix 2 (see The National Curriculum in England).

Spelling

National Curriculum objective	Working at greater depth
Use further prefixes and suffixes and understand the guidance for adding them.	Can correctly add a wide range of prefixes and suffixes and can use these words in their own writing.
Spell some words with 'silent' letters (for example, *knight*, *psalm*, *solemn*).	Can spell most words with silent letters encountered across Key Stage 2.
Continue to distinguish between homophones and other words which are often confused.	Can distinguish between an extensive range of homophones and other words which are often confused.
Use knowledge of morphology and etymology in spelling and understand that the spelling of some words needs to be learned specifically, as listed in English Appendix 1.	Can use their knowledge of morphology, etymology and unusual spelling to spell well.
Use dictionaries to check the spelling and meaning of words.	Can use a dictionary to check spelling and meaning, comparing the definition in different dictionaries if necessary.
Use the first three or four letters of a word to check spelling, meaning or both of these in a dictionary.	Can quickly locate words in a dictionary to check spelling and meaning, remembering many of these.
Use a thesaurus.	Can use a thesaurus to choose the best words for their writing.

Objective coverage overview

Unit	Objectives
1 Grammar: Word classes	To recognise nouns, adjectives, verbs, adverbs and adverbials. To use adjectives, adverbs and adverbials appropriately to modify nouns and verbs. To use adverbs to modify adjectives or other adverbs.
2 Grammar: Pronouns and determiners	To choose pronouns and possessive pronouns appropriately for clarity and cohesion and to avoid repetition. To use appropriate determiners, possessive determiners and demonstrative pronouns before nouns.
3 Grammar: Modal verbs and adverbs	To use modal verbs or adverbs to indicate degrees of possibility. To use modal verbs to indicate ability and obligation.
4 Grammar: Sentence types	To identify and use different sentence types, using correct punctuation.
5 Grammar: Conjunctions and subordinate clauses	To use co-ordinating conjunctions to link two words, phrases or clauses of equal importance. To use subordinating conjunctions to introduce subordinate clauses.
6 Grammar: Relative clauses	To use relative pronouns to introduce relative clauses. To understand that sometimes the relative pronoun can be omitted.
7 Grammar: Expanded noun phrases	To use expanded noun phrases to convey more information about a noun.
8 Grammar: Verb tenses	To use the simple present and past tenses, the present and past progressive tenses and the present and past perfect tenses correctly.
9 Grammar: Passive verbs	To use the passive form of verbs to affect the presentation of information in a sentence.
10 Punctuation: Brackets, dashes and commas	To use brackets, dashes and commas to indicate parenthesis.
11 Punctuation: Colons, semi-colons and dashes	To use colons, semi-colons or dashes to mark boundaries between independent clauses. To use a colon to introduce a list. To use semi-colons within lists.
12 Punctuation: Hyphens and commas to avoid ambiguity	To use hyphens to form compound words and to join prefixes to root words to avoid ambiguity. To use commas to avoid ambiguity.
13 Punctuation: Apostrophes to show contraction	To use apostrophes to contract words.
14 Punctuation: Apostrophes for possession	To use apostrophes to show possession.

Objective coverage overview

Unit	Objectives
15 Punctuation: Inverted commas	To use and punctuate direct speech using inverted commas.
16 Vocabulary: Prefixes	To add prefixes to root words to make new words.
17 Vocabulary: Suffixes	To use suffixes to change the class of a word.
18 Vocabulary: Antonyms and Synonyms	To understand how synonyms are related by meaning. To understand that antonyms are words that are opposite in meaning.
19 Vocabulary: Formal speech and writing	To recognise vocabulary and structures that are appropriate for formal speech and writing, including the subjunctive mood.
20 Spelling: Homophones and near-homophones	To spell homophones and near-homophones correctly.
21 Spelling: Etymology and morphology	To use knowledge of etymology and morphology to help in spelling and understanding of words.
22 Spelling: Tricky spellings	To spell words with silent letters. To spell words with the letter string 'ough'. To spell words with the /ee/ sound spelled 'ei' and 'ie' after 'c'.

Progression chart

Name: _____

Unit	Skills checked	Practised	Aimed higher!
1 Grammar: Word classes			
2 Grammar: Pronouns and determiners			
3 Grammar: Modal verbs and adverbs			
4 Grammar: Sentence types			
5 Grammar: Conjunctions and subordinate clauses			
6 Grammar: Relative clauses			
7 Grammar: Expanded noun phrases			
8 Grammar: Verb tenses			
9 Grammar: Passive verbs			
10 Punctuation: Brackets, dashes and commas			
11 Punctuation: Colons, semi-colons and dashes			
12 Punctuation: Hyphens and commas to avoid ambiguity			
13 Punctuation: Apostrophes to show contraction			
14 Punctuation: Apostrophes for possession			
15 Punctuation: Inverted commas			
16 Vocabulary: Prefixes			
17 Vocabulary: Suffixes			
18 Vocabulary: Synonyms and antonyms			
19 Vocabulary: Formal speech and writing			
20 Spelling: Homophones and near-homophones			
21 Spelling: Etymology and morphology			
22 Spelling: Tricky spellings			

Attendance chart

Subject: _____

Teacher: _____

Name	1	2	3	4	5	6	7	8	9	10	11	12	13	14	15	16	17	18	19	20	21	22

Dear Parents and Carers,

As you will be aware, towards the end of Year 6, the children will be sitting their National Curriculum (SATs) tests. This is obligatory for all children attending state schools and this year the tests will be taking place from _____ to _____. The tests the children will be sitting are:

English: Reading – 60 minutes

English: Grammar and Punctuation – 45 minutes

English: Spelling – approximately 15 minutes

Mathematics: Arithmetic – one paper, 40 minutes

Mathematics: Reasoning – two separate papers, 40 minutes each

The purpose of the tests is to monitor and compare the performance of state schools, but also to check on the abilities and progress of each child. Scores will continue to be used in secondary schools as a benchmark for future performance, and in some cases for sorting children into sets.

We are planning a series of Challenge sessions we would like your child to attend, if possible. These sessions will focus on deepening your child's understanding in a variety of areas and provide an opportunity for stretch and challenge. As such, the focus of these sessions will not generally be on explicit test practice. However, deep understanding and strong reasoning skills will be very beneficial when taking the tests.

Subject: _____

Dates: _____

Day(s): _____

Times: _____

If you are happy for your child to attend, please complete the form below and return it to us.

The best way to support your child through this period is to ensure that they get plenty of sleep and exercise, ensure they are not unduly worried about the tests, and that when they are doing homework they have a calm and quiet environment to work in. If you feel the need to do additional work with your child, please speak to us first so that we can work together and avoid duplication or confusion.

If there is anything else you would like us to clarify or provide further information on, please let us know.

With thanks for your support,

The Year 6 team

- -

Year 6 Challenge sessions

Child's name: _____

I give my permission for my child to attend the Challenge sessions.

Name: _____ Signed: _____

SCHOLASTIC

Reward Certificate

Well done!

I've aimed higher with SATs Challenge

Name: _____ Date: _____

My strongest areas are:

_____

_____

I will challenge myself to fly higher in:

_____

1

GRAMMAR

Word classes

Objectives

- To recognise nouns, adjectives, verbs, adverbs and adverbials.
- To use adjectives, adverbs and adverbials appropriately to modify nouns and verbs.
- To use adverbs to modify adjectives or other adverbs.

What the children need to know

- Common nouns are naming words for people, places, animals and things. They also name things that cannot be seen or touched, such as emotions (abstract nouns). Proper nouns name specific people, places, days of the week, months of the year, and always start with a capital letter.
- Adjectives modify nouns.
- A verb is a word for an action or a state of being.
- An adverb can modify a verb, saying more about manner, place, time or degree.
- An adverb can also modify an adjective or another adverb.
- An adverbial is a word or phrase that behaves like an adverb.

TEST LINKS:

Section 1:
Q1, 11, 14, 18, 33, 61, 62
Section 2, Word classes:
Q1, 2, 4, 5, 8
Section 3:
Q2, 11, 13, 16, 31, 34, 37

WORKBOOK LINKS:

Pages 6–7

⌲ Challenge and mastery ideas

- Provide children with photocopiable page 39 'Noun classification'. Children classify a selection of different common nouns and proper nouns and explain briefly their thinking, for example: *dog*– common noun, object/thing; *class* – common noun, collection of people; *health* – common noun, cannot be seen or touched (abstract); *Mount Everest, Sunday* – proper nouns.
- In pairs, children highlight nouns, adjectives, adverbs/adverbials and verbs in a text. Ensure they understand that *have, be* and *do* can act as auxiliary verbs (helping verbs) as well as main verbs.
- Provide children with sentences where an adverb modifies the verb but where another adverb could modify the adverb. For example: *Freddy worked _____ hard on his homework.* ⟶ *Freddy worked **really** hard on his homework.*
- Refer children to 'Writing activity 1' on photocopiable page 54.
- Give children sentences containing adverbials at the end and ask them to rewrite so that they start with the adverbial. For example: *We finally saw the exhibition after a long wait in the queue.* ⟶ *After a long wait in the queue, we finally saw the exhibition.*

⌲ Review

- Ask: *Are you confident identifying adverbs that can modify verbs by saying more about manner, place, time or degree? Can you give me an example of a sentence for each?*
- In guided reading sessions, ask: *What word class is...? How do you know?*

⌲ Watch and listen

- Children who are working confidently may point out that some adverbials contain prepositions; these are prepositional phrases acting as adverbials. For example: *I kicked my football **into the net**.*

2

Objectives

- To choose pronouns and possessive pronouns appropriately for clarity and cohesion and to avoid repetition.
- To use appropriate determiners, possessive determiners and demonstrative pronouns before nouns.

What the children need to know

- A pronoun can be used to replace a noun.
- A possessive pronoun replaces the possessor and the item possessed.
- A determiner is a word that introduces a noun. It goes before any modifiers, such as adjectives or other nouns.
- A possessive determiner indicates ownership of the noun in question.
- A demonstrative determiner can indicate the location or amount.

TEST LINKS:

Section 1:
Q18, 21, 24, 42, 48

Section 2,
Word classes: Q3, 6, 7

Section 3:
Q16, 18, 19, 25, 41, 46

WORKBOOK LINKS:

Pages 8–9

GRAMMAR
Pronouns and determiners

✈ Challenge and mastery ideas

- Hand out copies of photocopiable page 40 'Pronouns and determiners'. In the first section of the sheet, children are asked to replace the repeated nouns with appropriate pronouns.
- In the second section on the photocopiable page children should find as many examples as possible of pronouns, possessive pronouns, determiners, possessive determiners and demonstrative determiners. Ask them to use a colour code to highlight each type.
- Display a passage of text where pronouns are highlighted. Ask the children which nouns they refer to. For example: *The car sped past the children at an alarming speed. When **it** screamed to a stop, **they** looked at the driver. **He** put his head out of the window and asked **them** if **they** had seen his dog.*

✈ Review

- Ensure children are secure in identifying prepositions and using them. Some prepositions can also act as adverbs, depending on the context. For example: *I walked **down** the road* (preposition) *and I threw the book **down*** (adverb).

✈ Watch and listen

- More confident learners may grasp that the personal pronouns *I, you, she, he, it, we* and *they* are 'subject', whereas *me, him, her, it, us* and *them* are 'object'. Display the sentence: *She gave me the book.* Ask children to identify the pronoun which is the subject and the pronoun that is the object. Then give children sentences where the people's names can be replaced with a subject pronoun and an object pronoun. For example: *Samir told Grace to be quiet.* ⟶ *He told her to be quiet.*

3

Objectives

- To use modal verbs or adverbs to indicate degrees of possibility.
- To use modal verbs to indicate ability and obligation.

What the children need to know

- Modal verbs (*can, could, will, would, may, might, must, ought to, shall, should*) change the meaning of other verbs. They can indicate that an action is certain or uncertain, an ability to do something or an obligation.
- A modal verb is followed by a verb in its basic form (the infinitive).
- Some adverbs can indicate that an action is certain or uncertain.

TEST LINKS:

Section 1: Q14, 20, 50

Section 2, Verb forms, tense and consistency: Q6, 9

Section 3: Q21

WORKBOOK LINKS:

Pages 10–11

GRAMMAR

Modal verbs and adverbs

✒ Challenge and mastery ideas

- In pairs, children write a sentence containing a modal verb that indicates possibility or certainty. They swap with another pair who decides whether the intention is to show possibility or certainty.
- In pairs, one child writes a sentence containing an adverb to show certainty, while the other writes a sentence containing an adverb to show uncertainty.
- Give children photocopiable page 41 'Degrees of possibility'. Ask them to write in the correct columns all the modal verbs and adverbs they can think of that belong under the headings 'Uncertain', 'Possible', 'Probable' and 'Certain'.
- In groups, children work together to make a list of things most 10- and 11-year-olds might do, ought to do and can do.

✒ Review

- Ask: *Can you use modal verbs and/or adverbs to indicate degrees of possibility in your writing? Can you give me an example of a sentence that shows certainty using an adverb?*
- Ask: *Can you give me a sentence containing a modal verb that shows an obligation?*
- Ask: *Can you give me a sentence containing the adverb* **perhaps**? *Consider where you would put it in your sentence.*

✒ Watch and listen

- Give children who are working confidently two sentences where the modal verb **can** has two different intentions. For example: *He can run two miles without stopping.* (certain) *There can be up to 70 children in the pool at one time.* (possible) Ask them to explain the difference in meaning.

4

Sentence types

Objectives

- To identify and use different sentence types, using correct punctuation.

What the children need to know

- A statement is a sentence that tells you something. It ends with a full stop.
- A question is a sentence that asks something. A question can be a statement followed by a comma and a question tag. (*You're ten, aren't you?*) It ends with a question mark.
- A command is a sentence that tells you to do something. It contains a command verb (an imperative), often at the beginning of the sentence. It ends with either a full stop or an exclamation mark.
- An exclamation is a sentence where surprise, shock, pain or a strong emotion is expressed. It starts with *How* or *What* and contains a subject and a verb. It ends with an exclamation mark.

TEST LINKS:

Section 1:
Q4, 10, 28, 30
Section 2,
Functions of sentences:
Q1, 2, 3, 5, 6
Section 3: Q5, 12

WORKBOOK LINKS:

Pages 12–13

Challenge and mastery ideas

- Give pairs of children a range of answers and ask them to write suitable questions to generate those answers. Swap with other pairs who ensure that each question starts with a capital letter and ends with a question mark.
- Children write instructions for a recipe or a board game. Ask them to highlight the command – or imperative – verbs that they have used. *Can you explain why we use command sentences?*
- Children write factual statements about a topic area they are learning (for example, history or geography).
- On the whiteboard, display the words *shock, surprise, thrilled, scared* and *fright*. Children use these words to create exclamation sentences. For example: *How shocked I was when the lights went out! What a thrill it was when our team won the final!*
- Refer children to 'Writing activity 2' on photocopiable page 54.

Review

- Ask: *What are the two different punctuation marks that can come at the end of a command? Can you write an example of each?*
- Ask: *What type of verbs are used in a command sentence?*
- Ask: *Can you give me an example of a question with a question tag?*

Watch and listen

- Give children some basic information, such as *Michael plays the piano*. Ask them to use this to make a statement, a question, a command and an exclamation. Look out for children who show a depth of understanding by being able to explain confidently how they used this information and why they chose to use these different types of sentence.

5

Objectives

- To use co-ordinating conjunctions to link two words, phrases or clauses of equal importance.
- To use subordinating conjunctions to introduce subordinate clauses.

What the children need to know

- A co-ordinating conjunction, such as *and, but, or,* links two words, phrases or clauses of equal importance.
- A subordinate clause is introduced by a subordinating conjunction such as *because, even though.*
- A subordinate clause is dependent on a main clause for sense; it doesn't make sense on its own.
- A clause always contains a subject and a verb, and a main clause makes sense on its own.

TEST LINKS:

Section 1:
Q17, 18, 27, 55

Section 2,
Combining words phrases and clauses:
Q1, 2, 3, 5

Section 3: Q15, 20, 23

WORKBOOK LINKS:

Pages 14–15

GRAMMAR

Conjunctions and subordinate clauses

◢ Challenge and mastery ideas

- Give children sentences where co-ordinating conjunctions have been used incorrectly. For example: *My brother doesn't like water but milk. I wanted to stay up late and Mum said it was time for bed.* Invite them to rewrite the sentences, using the correct co-ordinating conjunction.
- Give children photocopiable page 42 'Conjunction word cards' and ask them to cut out the conjunctions into separate word cards. Place the cards face down on the table and ask children to take it in turns with a partner to choose a card and make up a sentence using the conjunction.
- Display subordinate clauses and ask children to create suitable main clauses to make full sentences. For example:

  _____ *after he had brushed his teeth.*

  _____ *before it was too late.*
- Refer children to 'Writing activity 3' on photocopiable page 55.

◢ Review

- In guided reading sessions, ask: *Can you identify a subordinating conjunction that introduces a subordinate clause? Can you identify the main clause?*
- Alternate with: *Can you identify a subordinate clause which is dependent on a main clause?*
- Display a subordinate clause such as *...unless we were well behaved.* Ask children to complete the sentence by adding a main clause to make a 'silly sentence'. For example: *We knew our trip to the North Pole would be cancelled unless we were well behaved.*

◢ Watch and listen

- Ask: *Is the word **after** used as a subordinating conjunction in this sentence:* We went to bed after supper. *Why not?* Elicit that here, *after* is used as a preposition. *How do you know it is not a subordinating conjunction in this instance?* Elicit that there is no verb in *after supper.*

6

Relative clauses

Objectives

- To use relative pronouns to introduce relative clauses.
- To understand that sometimes the relative pronoun can be omitted.

What the children need to know

- A relative clause, which is a type of subordinate clause, is often introduced by a relative pronoun such as *who* or *that*.
- Sometimes, the relative pronoun is omitted, so it is implied.
- A relative clause is used to define the noun that comes before it.
- A relative clause can also begin with the adverbs *when* and *where*.

TEST LINKS:

Section 1: Q5, 16

Section 2, Combining words, phrases and clauses: Q6

Section 3: Q3, 15, 16, 19, 56

WORKBOOK LINKS:

Pages 16–17

◀ Challenge and mastery ideas

- Hand out copies of photocopiable page 43 'Who, whom, whose?' and ask the children to cut out the relative pronouns into separate cards. Tell them to place the cards face down on the table, take it in turns with a partner to choose a card and make up a sentence using the relative pronoun.
- Using the sentences created above, children work with a partner to establish which sentences make sense when the relative pronoun is omitted.
- Explain that the relative pronoun *whom* is used rather than *who* when it is the object of a verb or preposition. *Whom did she marry? The man with whom...* It isn't always used in everyday speech and writing as it is considered quite formal. Provide children with sentences that require the relative pronouns *who* or *whom*. For example: *The man with _____ my father has formed a business is called Charles Brown. The man _____ has formed a business with my father is called Charles Brown.* With a partner, children decide which relative pronoun to use.

◀ Review

- In guided reading sessions, ask: *Can you identify a sentence containing a relative clause beginning with a relative pronoun? Could the relative pronoun be omitted? If not, explain why.*
- Ask: *Can you give me an example of when **whom** is used instead of **who?*** (For example: *To whom did you give your homework? Whom did you call?*)
- Remind children that relative clauses can also begin with the adverbs *when* and *where*.

◀ Watch and listen

- Display the following sentences: *The girls **who** won the netball stood up to be applauded. Some of the people **that** use our park are litterbugs.* Ask children what they think the difference between the sentences is. Elicit that the first sentence uses the relative pronoun *who* and the second sentence uses *that*. Can they explain why? Elicit that we use *who* for people but *that* can be used for people when we are being unspecific.
- Display the following sentences: *The dog **which** was running wild has been caught. My cat, **who** is called Tabby, always purrs when she sees me.* Ask children what they think the difference between the sentences is. Elicit that the first sentence uses the relative pronoun *which* and the second sentence uses *who*. Can they explain why? Elicit that we generally use *which* for animals but *who* for a pet.

7

Objectives

- To use expanded noun phrases to convey more information about a noun.

What the children need to know

- A noun phrase is a phrase that is about a noun.
- An expanded noun phrase includes more information about the noun.
- The noun might be modified by an adjective, another noun and/ or a preposition phrase.

TEST LINKS:

Section 1: Q33, 49

Section 2, Combining words, phrases and clauses: Q4

Section 3: Q38

WORKBOOK LINKS:

Pages 18–19

GRAMMAR

Expanded noun phrases

✈ Challenge and mastery ideas

- Hand out copies of photocopiable page 44 'Tell me more!'. Children are asked to expand a selection of noun phrases by adding further information about each noun. Share and discuss their expanded noun phrases as a group.
- Expand the activity above to include preposition phrases. For example: *The grumpy old man with the bald head.*
- In guided reading, ask children to expand noun phrases that they come across to make the noun more interesting/give more information about the noun.

✈ Review

- Ask: *Can you suggest how to make the displayed expanded noun phrases even better?*
- Play 'Add a word, change a word' where children add, for example, an interesting adjective, and change, for example, an existing adjective for a more interesting one.

✈ Watch and listen

- Give children a range of nouns. Ask them to create noun phrases, then expand these and then expand further. For example: *field* ⟶ *the field* ⟶ *the flowery fields* ⟶ *the flowery fields stretching as far as the eye could see.* Look out for children who are able to suggest imaginative/interesting adjectives and phrases in this activity.

8

GRAMMAR
Verb tenses

Objectives

- To use the simple present and past tenses, the present and past progressive tenses and the present and past perfect tenses correctly.

What the children need to know

- How to form the simple present and past tense and when to use it.
- How to form the present and past progressive tense and when to use it.
- How to form the present and past perfect tense and when to use it.

TEST LINKS:

Section 1:
Q2, 8, 35, 43, 46, 52, 61

Section 2,
Verb forms, tense and consistency:
Q1, 3, 4, 10

Section 3:
Q1, 10, 40, 45, 48, 50, 52

WORKBOOK LINKS:

Pages 20–23

✦ Challenge and mastery ideas

- Children write a diary entry or blog post about what they did at the weekend or on holiday. Working with a partner, they should then discuss the range of past tenses they have used. For example: *I **walked** on the beach every morning. One day, as we **were fishing** off the rocks, we **saw** some dolphins.*
- Give children a table with the following headings:

	Simple present	Simple past	Present progressive	Past progressive	Present perfect	Past perfect
How it is formed						
Example						

- Write how each tense is formed. Then write an example sentence for each verb form. (See verb tenses table on page 20 of the *Workbook*.)
- Refer children to 'Writing activity 4' on photocopiable page 55'.

✦ Review

- Extend the activity above by asking children to explain when the present and past progressive tenses and the present and past perfect tenses are used.
- Ask: *What is wrong with this sentence: One day, as we **fished** off the rocks, we **were seeing** some dolphins.*

✦ Watch and listen

- Children should be aware that the verb 'to have' can be both an auxiliary verb and a main verb. Ask: *Can you give an example sentence for each?* For example: *We have eaten too much chocolate.* ('have' as an auxiliary used to form present perfect.) *I have two brothers and a sister.* ('have' as a main verb.)
- Display the following sentences: *Tom ran towards the truck while it was driving away. Tom was running towards the truck when it drove away.* Ask: *Can you explain the differences between the verb tenses in each sentence?* Children showing a greater depth of understanding should be able to describe the subtle differences.
- Watch for children who understand why we don't use progressive tenses with certain verbs, (such as *believe, trust, know*).

9

Objectives

- To use the passive form of verbs to affect the presentation of information in a sentence.

What the children need to know

- Writing in the active voice means that the subject of the sentence is 'doing' or 'being' something and, if there is an object, the object is what the subject is 'acting upon'.

- The noun, pronoun or noun phrase that normally would be the object in the active-voice sentence becomes the subject of the passive-voice sentence.

- The passive voice is formed by a combination of the verb 'to be' + the past participle of the main verb.

TEST LINKS:

Section 1: Q29, 53

Section 2,
Verb forms, tense and consistency: Q2, 8

Section 3: Q27, 55

WORKBOOK LINKS:

Pages 20–23

GRAMMAR

Passive verbs

 Challenge and mastery ideas

- Give children photocopiable page 45 'From active to passive', which shows a selection of sentences in the active voice. Ask them to highlight the subject and object in each sentence, then rewrite it in the passive voice.

- Using their guided reading books or another text, children note active and passive sentences in a two-column table.

- Create a selection of passive-voice sentences on strips of paper. Cut them up into subject, verb and agent. Shuffle the strips of paper, then ask children in pairs to put them together to make full sentences. Once they have done this, ask them to write them in the active voice.

- Ask children to consider why the passive voice is preferable in some contexts. Elicit that in the passive voice, the emphasis is on the person (or object) that experiences the action rather than the person (or object) that performs the action. Share an example which emphasises this – for example: *A house painter painted the house yesterday.* Ask them to change the sentence into the passive voice: *The house was painted yesterday.* Challenge the children to think of some of their own examples, and write them in the active and the passive voice.

- The passive voice is also often used in formal contexts. For example: *"You are most warmly welcomed to our Year 6 summer performance," said the head teacher.* Ask children to think of some signs they could put up around the school and decide whether they would work best in the passive or active voice.

 Review

- Ask: *Can you tell me how the passive voice is formed? Can you give me an example?*

- Ask: *Can you give me an example of a formal sentence written in the passive voice?*

Watch and listen

- Ask: *Is the agent always necessary in a passive-voice sentence?* Elicit that it isn't always required. For example: *The thieves were pursued **(by the police)**. He was soaked **(by the rain)** because he forgot his umbrella.* Listen for children who can give an example sentence and are able to explain clearly why the agent isn't required.

- Watch for children who make sensible choices between active and passive voice in their writing.

10

Objectives

- To use brackets, dashes and commas to indicate parenthesis.

What the children need to know

- Brackets, dashes and commas can be used to indicate parenthesis.
- Parenthesis means inserting a word, phrase or clause as an explanation or afterthought into a sentence that would still make sense without it. The word, phrase or clause sits inside a pair of brackets, dashes or commas.
- Dashes and commas can only come inside a sentence, whereas brackets can come either inside or at the end of the sentence.

TEST LINKS:

Section 1: Q15, 26, 54
Section 2, Punctuation: Q2, 5, 9
Section 3: Q17, 32, 51, 53

WORKBOOK LINKS:

Pages 26–27

PUNCTUATION

Brackets, dashes and commas

✈ Challenge and mastery ideas

- Provide children with copies of photocopiable page 46 'Scrambled sentences'. Ask them to cut out each sentence into three separate strips and shuffle them. Then ask them to cut out the pairs of punctuation marks provided at the bottom of the photocopiable page. Children put each sentence in the correct order, inserting the missing punctuation to indicate parenthesis.
- Give children sentences where the brackets, dashes and commas have been placed incorrectly. With a partner, they use a different coloured pen to put them in the correct places.
- Display sentences that could be followed by an explanation or afterthought and ask children to add a word, phrase or clause in brackets to finish off the sentence. For example: *Gran was really pleased with her new blue hair colour* ⟶ *Gran was really pleased with her new blue hair colour (personally, I thought it looked very odd).*

✈ Review

- Ask: *Can you explain what parenthesis is? Can you tell me the different punctuation marks that can be used to indicate that a word, phrase or clause is in parenthesis? Can you give me an example of a sentence where a word, phrase or clause is in parenthesis?*

✈ Watch and listen

- Watch for children who use the full range of punctuation to indicate parenthesis. Also, look out for those who use brackets at the end of a sentence and punctuate correctly, by using the full stop outside the final bracket.

11

Objectives

- To use colons, semi-colons or dashes to mark boundaries between independent clauses.
- To use a colon to introduce a list.
- To use semi-colons within lists.

What the children need to know

- A colon can be used after a clause and before another clause that explains or gives more detail about the first.
- A colon can introduce a list.
- A semi-colon can be used to link two closely related sentences.
- A semi-colon can be used to separate items in a list that consist of more than one word.
- A dash can be used to show a break or pause in a sentence, to add suspense or show a change in direction in the sentence.

TEST LINKS:

Section 1: Q9

Section 2, Punctuation: Q3, 7, 9

Section 3: Q6, 29, 32

WORKBOOK LINKS:

Pages 28–29

PUNCTUATION

Colons, semi-colons and dashes

✎ Challenge and mastery ideas

- Ask children to name some book titles and their authors. Display these on the whiteboard. For example:
  - *Harry Potter and the Philosopher's Stone* by J K Rowling
  - *The Boy in the Striped Pyjamas* by John Boyne
  - *Mortal Chaos* by Matt Dickinson
  - *The Diary of a Young Girl* by Anne Frank
- Now ask the children to introduce the list of books with a sentence ending with a colon and using semi-colons rather than commas to separate the items. (For example, The following books can be found in our library: xxxx; xxxx; …)
- In a guided reading session, ask children to find two closely related sentences in their book that could be rewritten as one, linked with a semi-colon.
- Present children with sentences, then ask them for a second sentence that explains or gives more detail about the first, linking the two with a colon. For example:
  - *My clothing wasn't very appropriate for the wedding.*
  - *My clothing wasn't very appropriate for the wedding: my scruffy boots, an old T-shirt and jeans did not endear me to the bride's family.*

✎ Review

- Ask: *Can you explain how colons, semi-colons and dashes can be used to mark boundaries between independent clauses? Can you give me an example?*
- Ask: *How else can a dash be used? How else can a semi-colon be used? How else can a colon be used?*
- Ask: *What is the difference between a dash and hyphen?*

✎ Watch and listen

- Watch for children who use colons, semi-colons and dashes appropriately, to mark the boundary between independent clauses, and thus vary their writing in both fiction and non-fiction.

12

PUNCTUATION

Hyphens and commas to avoid ambiguity

Objectives

- To use hyphens to form compound words and to join prefixes to root words to avoid ambiguity.
- To use commas to avoid ambiguity.

What the children need to know

- Ambiguity is where a word or sentence can have more than one meaning.
- Hyphens can be used in compound words to avoid ambiguity.
- Hyphens can be used to join prefixes to root words to avoid ambiguity.
- Commas can be used to avoid ambiguity.

TEST LINKS:

Section 1: Q25

Section 2, Punctuation: Q5; Vocabulary: Q7

Section 3: Q43

WORKBOOK LINKS:

Pages 30–31

✎ Challenge and mastery ideas

- Hand out copies of photocopiable page 47 'What does it mean?' which shows pairs of words that can start with either the prefix 're-' (with hyphen) or 're' (no hyphen). Using a dictionary, children write definitions for each word.
- Give children sentences where the omission/inclusion of a comma (or commas) affects the meaning. Ask them to explain the difference in meaning. For example:
  ○ *Writing clearly isn't easy. Writing, clearly, isn't easy.*
  ○ *I didn't fall thankfully. I didn't fall, thankfully.*
  ○ *I ate, Susan. I ate Susan.*
- Ask children to write a sentence of their own where the omission of a comma (or commas) affects the meaning. Then ask them to write the same sentence, this time including a comma (or commas) to affect the meaning.

✎ Review

- Ask: *Can you explain what ambiguity is?*
- Ask: *Can you explain the different meanings of words with a hyphenated prefix and non-hyphenated prefix? What examples can you give?*
- Ask: *Can you explain how the inclusion of a comma can affect the meaning of a sentence? Where else do we use a comma in writing?* Elicit that we use commas in lists and after fronted adverbials, and a pair of commas can be used to indicate parenthesis. They can also be used after direct speech, before the final inverted commas, or after the information about who is speaking, if this comes before the direct speech.

✎ Watch and listen

- Watch for children who can confidently differentiate between a hyphen and a dash, and who can explain the difference in meaning between non-hyphenated words and words where a hyphen is used to join a prefix to the root word.
- Listen to children using the word 'ambiguity' correctly, with an understanding of how a hyphen and a comma can be used to avoid ambiguity.

13

Objectives

- To use apostrophes to contract words.

What the children need to know

- Apostrophes can be used to show where a letter, or letters, have been omitted in order to contract a word or words.
- An apostrophe is shaped like a comma but sits at the same height as inverted commas.
- The apostrophe is positioned exactly above where the omitted letter, or letters, would be.

PUNCTUATION

Apostrophes to show contraction

✈ Challenge and mastery ideas

- Provide children with photocopiable page 48 'Missing apostrophes' which shows a passage where no apostrophes have been used in contractions. Ask them to highlight the relevant words, then rewrite the passage correctly on the lines below.
- Now ask children to write the full form of each word in the activity above.
- Ask children to use the internet to investigate why *will not* becomes *won't* (from the Old English verb *willan* meaning *will*.)
- In groups of four, one pair of children has a short conversation. The remaining pair writes down the contracted word forms they hear as they listen to the conversation. Then swap.

✈ Review

- Ask: *Can you tell me what letter or letters in the contractions **doesn't** and **should've** have been replaced by the apostrophe?*
- Invite a volunteer to come to the whiteboard and place an apostrophe in the contractions *doesn't* and *should've* in the correct position and at the correct height.

✈ Watch and listen

- Watch for children using correctly contracted words, confidently writing the apostrophe at the correct height and position.

TEST LINKS:

Section 1: Q3, 45, 56
Section 2, Punctuation: Q6, 10
Section 3: Q4, 47, 53

WORKBOOK LINKS:

Pages 32–33

14

Objectives

- To use apostrophes to show possession.

What the children need to know

- An apostrophe can be used to show that something belongs to someone or something.

- The apostrophe must be positioned exactly between the final letter of the word and the letter 's' in singular nouns and immediately after the 's' in regular plural nouns ending in 's'. In irregular plural nouns, the apostrophe comes between the final letter and the letter 's'.

- The apostrophe comes after the final 's' of proper nouns ending in 's' followed by an 's'.

TEST LINKS:

Section 1: Q3, 56

Section 2, Punctuation: Q8, 10

Section 3: Q4, 39, 44, 53

WORKBOOK LINKS:

Pages 34-35

PUNCTUATION

Apostrophes for possession

✒ Challenge and mastery ideas

- Display sentences containing a list of people or things that 'own' things. Provide some tricky examples, using collective nouns for the possessor and abstract nouns for the possession. Ask the children to say who the possessor is. For example: *The class's behaviour had been exemplary. Our team's victory will go down in history*.

- Provide children with photocopiable page 49 'It's mine!' The top half of the sheet provides a list of nouns alongside a list of singular people or nouns that could 'own' these nouns. Ask the children to turn the words into phrases (or expanded noun phrases) to show possession.

- On the bottom half of the photocopiable page is a list of plural people or nouns that could 'own' singular or plural nouns. As in the activity above, invite the children to turn them into phrases (or expanded noun phrases) to show possession.

✒ Review

- Display a sentence which shows ownership using an apostrophe to indicate possession. Ask: *Can you say who the owner is in this sentence?*

- Display two sentences where the apostrophes used to indicate possession are in the wrong place. Ask: *Can you tell me what is wrong with each sentence?*

- Display a sentence in which an apostrophe to indicate possession has been omitted. Invite a volunteer to come to the whiteboard and place an apostrophe in this sentence, in the correct position and at the correct height.

✒ Watch and listen

- Watch for children who show understanding that *it's* always means *it is* or *it has* – there is no apostrophe in the possessive form *its*.

15

Inverted commas

Objectives
- To use and punctuate direct speech using inverted commas.

What the children need to know
- Inverted commas are used to show where spoken words start and finish in direct speech.
- Inverted commas can be used for quotations and quotes.
- The opening inverted commas should look like back-to-front and upside-down commas. The closing inverted commas should look like normal commas.
- Closing inverted commas must come after the final punctuation mark.
- Inverted commas need to be placed at the same height as a capital letter or ascender.
- Inverted commas can be either 'single' or "double".

✈ Challenge and mastery ideas
- Present children with direct speech where the inverted commas have been incorrectly placed. Ask them to explain why they are incorrect.
- Provide children with a short passage containing direct speech but where there are no punctuation marks. Ask children to insert all the missing punctuation.
- On the whiteboard, display sentences written as reported speech (for example, reports by witnesses in a newspaper article). Ask children to rewrite the sentences as direct speech, making the appropriate verb and person changes. For example: *One eyewitness said she saw the man running towards the outskirts of town.* ⟶ *"I saw the man running towards the outskirts of town," said one eyewitness.*
- Refer children to 'Writing activity 5' on photocopiable page 56.

✈ Review
- Display two sentences where the inverted commas are in the wrong place. For example: *"When will you be finished"? asked the teacher. "Soon", replied Sam.* Ask: *Can you tell me what is wrong with each sentence? Where should the inverted commas be in each case?*
- Display a sentence where the inverted commas have been omitted. Invite a volunteer to come to the whiteboard and place the inverted commas in the correct position and at the correct height.

✈ Watch and listen
- Watch for children positioning inverted commas correctly, at the right height.

TEST LINKS:

Section 1: Q22
Section 2, Punctuation: Q4
Section 3: Q24

WORKBOOK LINKS:

Pages 36–37

16

VOCABULARY
Prefixes

Objectives
- To add prefixes to root words to make new words.

What the children need to know
- Most prefixes are added to the beginning of root words without any changes in spelling.
- Some prefixes come from Greek and Latin.
- Some prefixes can be hyphenated to the root word.

 Challenge and mastery ideas

- Display the prefix 're', which usually means to repeat or to do again. Ask children to write as many words as they can think of that start with this prefix.
- Display the words *represent* and *re-present* and ask children what the difference in meaning is. Elicit that *represent* means *to act for someone* and the hyphenated word *re-present* means *to present again*. Ask children to explain the difference in meaning between similar pairs of words – for example, *recover/re-cover, resort/re-sort, repress/re-press* Discuss how prefixes change the meaning of the root word they are added to and that, as well as 're-', there are other prefixes that can change the meaning of a root word so that it means the opposite.
- Provide children with photocopiable page 50 'Opposite meanings'. Ask them to complete the grid by adding the appropriate negative prefix ('un', 'dis', 'mis', 'il', 'ir', 'im' and 'in') to each word listed. To increase the challenge, they could play it as a game against the clock. Provide dictionaries if necessary.
- Display prefixes of Greek and Latin origin and ask children for words that they know starting with these (for example, 'sub', 'trans', 'auto'). Gather suggestions, group accordingly, then ask children for the meaning of each prefix.
- Investigate words that use Greek and Latin number prefixes, such as 'uni', 'bi', 'dec' and 'cent'. What words do they know using these prefixes?

Review

- Ask: *What is the difference in meaning between* **resign** *and* **re-sign**?
- Ask: *What spelling rule can you tell me for the prefix 'im'?* Elicit that it comes at the start of words beginning with 'm' or 'p' (for example, *immature, imperfect*).

Watch and listen

- Listen to children explain the difference in meaning between similar pairs of words – for example, *recover/re-cover, resort/re-sort, repress/re-press*.
- Watch for children who can demonstrate understanding of a range of different prefixes and how they change the meaning of the root words they are added to.

TEST LINKS:

Section 1: Q7, 12, 23, 58

Section 2, Vocabulary: Q3, 5

Section 3: Q8, 14, 54, 58

WORKBOOK LINKS:

Pages 38–39

17

Objectives

- To use suffixes to change the class of a word.

What the children need to know

- Some verbs can be changed into adjectives and adverbs by adding suffixes.
- Some verbs can be changed into nouns by adding suffixes.
- Some nouns can be changed into adjectives by adding suffixes.
- Some adjectives can be changed into nouns by adding suffixes.
- When adding a suffix starting with a vowel to words ending in 'fer', the 'r' is doubled if the syllable 'fer' is still stressed after the suffix is added.

TEST LINKS:

Section 1: Q19, 36, 41

Section 2,
Word classes: Q5;
Vocabulary: Q6, 8, 11

Section 3: Q22

WORKBOOK LINKS:

Pages 40–41

VOCABULARY
Suffixes

✦ Challenge and mastery ideas

- Provide children with sentences to complete where they must change verbs into adjectives or adverbs by adding an appropriate suffix. For example:
  - ○ *Mum is very* _____ (observe) *when it comes to me washing the dishes.*
  - ○ *Mr Naismith was* _____ (understand) *cross with Keannan who kept interrupting.*
- Call out 'fer' words for children to spell correctly according to the spelling rule. For example:

transfer	transferred	transference
prefer	preferred	preference
confer	conferred	conference
refer	referred	reference

- Ask children to create a list of suffixes they know. Provide children with photocopiable page 51 'Which suffix?' Invite them to use appropriate suffixes to change each verb in the table into a noun, and then change the nouns into adjectives. In the second part of the activity on the sheet, children are asked to change a list of adjectives into nouns.

✦ Review

- Ask: *Can you tell me and spell the noun you can make from the adjective* **pretty**?
- Ask: *Can you tell me and spell the noun you can make from the verb* **acquaint**?
- Ask: *Can you tell me and spell the adverb you can make from the verb* **understand**?
- Ask: *Can you tell me and spell the noun you can make from the adjective* **pregnant**?

✦ Watch and listen

- Watch for children adding suffixes to words, choosing confidently between 'ible' and 'able', 'ance' and 'ence', 'ibly' and 'ably', 'ancy' and 'ency'.
- Similarly, are children using their understanding of the spelling rule for 'fer' words to either double the 'r' or not?

18

Objectives

- To understand how synonyms are related by meaning.
- To understand that antonyms are words that are opposite in meaning.

What the children need to know

- Synonyms are words that have the same (or almost the same) meaning.
- When choosing a synonym, make sure the meaning fits the context of the sentence.
- Antonyms are words that are opposite in meaning.
- Many antonyms are made by adding a negative prefix to the root word.

TEST LINKS:

Section 1: Q7, 12, 23, 51

Section 2, Vocabulary: Q1, 2, 5, 10

Section 3: Q8, 49

WORKBOOK LINKS:

Pages 42–43

VOCABULARY

Synonyms and antonyms

✈ Challenge and mastery ideas

- In guided reading sessions, ask children to replace the word *said* when it appears as part of direct speech with a suitable synonym.
- Refer back to the negative prefixes covered on page 32 ('un', 'dis', 'mis', 'il', 'ir', 'im' and 'in'). Display a range of words, each of which can be made opposite in meaning by adding one of these negative prefixes.
- Provide children with photocopiable page 52 'That doesn't sound right!', where the words in bold in the text do not make sense in the context of the sentence. Ask them to write the most suitable antonym above each one.

✈ Review

- Ask: *What sort of book would you use to find a synonym or an antonym?*
- Ask: *Can you explain what a synonym is? Can you give me a synonym for the word **diligent**?*
- Ask: *Can you explain what an antonym is? Can you give me an antonym for the word **reluctant**?*
- Ask: *Which prefix would you add to the word **probable** to make it opposite in meaning?*

✈ Watch and listen

- Watch for children independently referring to a thesaurus to find suitable synonyms and antonyms.
- Also, look out for children who choose the correct prefix to create antonyms.

19

Objectives

- To recognise vocabulary and structures that are appropriate for formal speech and writing, including the subjunctive mood.

What the children need to know

- In formal speech and writing, correct grammar (or Standard English) is used, as well as more formal vocabulary.
- The subjunctive mood can be used in formal speech and writing.
- Informal speech and writing is a relaxed, chatty way of speaking and writing. It might include non-Standard English such as *I done* and *You was*, as well as Standard English (correct grammar).

TEST LINKS:

Section 1: Q13, 34, 44

Section 2, Standard English and formality: Q1, 2, 3, 4, 5, 6

Section 3: Q9, 30, 36

WORKBOOK LINKS:

Pages 44–45

VOCABULARY

Formal speech and writing

✒ Challenge and mastery ideas

- Ask children for some 'text speak' phrases and display. For example: *C U l8r Wot you doin 2nite?* Ask them to write them out in Standard English, such as: *I'll see you later. What are you doing tonight?*
- Display the following writing genres on the whiteboard:
  - teenager's personal diary
  - letter to the head teacher
  - postcard to your parents
  - text to your best friend
  - politician's speech
- Ask them to say whether each example would be formal or informal. Discuss which might use non-Standard English.
- Provide children with formal sentences that need completing using the subjunctive mood. For example, *If you _____ to vote for me, I can assure you that you won't regret it.*
- Ask children to write a short information text about something that they are interested in (such as cycling). They should include subject-specific vocabulary to show that they are an 'expert'.
- Refer children to 'Writing activity 6' on photocopiable page 56.

✒ Review

- Invite children to discuss with a partner how they would start a formal letter to the head teacher asking him/her to consider changing the school's uniform policy. Ask: *What examples of formal vocabulary did you use?*
- Invite children to write a brief, chatty postcard to a friend describing a place they are visiting. Ask: *What examples of informal vocabulary did you use?*

✒ Watch and listen

- Watch for children choosing to use the passive voice in formal speech and writing (such as *I have been invited by your head teacher to give a presentation about...*) and using high-level and subject-specific vocabulary.

20

Objectives

- To spell homophones and near-homophones correctly.

What the children need to know

- Homophones are words that sound the same but have a different meaning and spelling.
- Near-homophones are words that sound *almost* the same but have a different meaning and spelling.

TEST LINKS:

Section 1,
Spelling: Q18, 19

Section 2,
Vocabulary: Q9

Section 3,
Spelling: Q6

WORKBOOK LINKS:

Pages 46–47

SPELLING

Homophones and near-homophones

Challenge and mastery ideas

- Present children with a blank grid to create their own crossword puzzle. The clues (across and down) are for pairs of homophones and near-homophones. For example: not moving (*stationary*); writing/office materials (*stationery*). Children swap with each other to complete the crossword.
- Provide children with photocopiable page 53 'Sounds the same'. Ask them to look at the list of words on the sheet and to write in their homophones/near-homophones as well as definitions. More confident learners could include the word class of the homophones/near-homophones.

Review

- Ask: *Can you tell me the difference between homophones and near-homophones? Can you give me an example of each?*
- Ask: *Can you give me the different meanings of each of the following homophones: raise, rays and raze?*

Watch and listen

- Watch for children who can confidently make accurate choices between pairs/groups of homophones and near-homophones in all their writing, creating their own strategies to help them in their choices if necessary.

21

Objectives

- To use knowledge of etymology and morphology to help in spelling and understanding of words.

What the children need to know

- Etymology is the study of the origin of words and how they have changed over time.
- The morphology of a word is how it is structured internally in terms of root words and suffixes or prefixes, as well as other changes (such as *mouse* to *mice*).

SPELLING

Etymology and morphology

◢ Challenge and mastery ideas

- Provide children with the root 'graph'. How many words containing this root can they think of? Elicit the words *telegraph, grapheme, photograph, paragraph, autograph*. Ask the children what this root means.
- Provide children with Latin and Greek roots such as 'deca', 'finis' and 'annus'. Ask them to write as many words as possible that are derived from these roots.
- Display the root word 'port' which is of Latin origin. Explain that it means to carry, bring or bear but can be changed by adding different prefixes and suffixes. Now display the prefixes 'trans', 'de', 'ex', 'im', 're', 'tele' and 'un' and the suffixes 'able', 'ment', 'er', 'ation', 'ance', 'ee' and 'ant'. Ask the children to make a new word from the root 'port' by adding a prefix or a suffix (or a combination of both).

◢ Review

- Ask: *If <u>monos</u> is Greek for 'alone or single', what does* **monosyllabic** *mean? What does* **monochrome** *mean?*
- Ask: *If <u>bene</u> is Latin for 'well', what does* **beneficial** *mean? What does* **benevolent** *mean?*

◢ Watch and listen

- Ensure children are aware of other words that have been borrowed from other languages, such as *caravan* from Persian, *yacht* from Dutch, *cul-de-sac* from French and *pizza* from Italian. Watch for children who identify more obvious examples of these words and encourage them to investigate these words' origins.

TEST LINKS:

Section 1: Q41
Section 2, Vocabulary: Q4

WORKBOOK LINKS:

Pages 48–49

22

SPELLING
Tricky spellings

Objectives

- To spell words with silent letters.
- To spell words with the letter string 'ough'.
- To spell words with the /ee/ sound spelled 'ie' and 'ei' after 'c'.

What the children need to know

- Some words have silent letters which are letters that are not pronounced.
- The letter string 'ough' can be used for a number of different sounds.
- For words that contain a long /ee/ sound, the spelling is usually 'ie', except when it comes after 'c'.
- There are exceptions to this rule.

✈ Challenge and mastery ideas

- Provide children with a mixture of words containing different silent letters (such as *whistle, sign, science, write, calf*). Challenge them to write as many other words as they can think of containing the same silent letter.
- Give children sentences where words that should contain the letter string 'ough' have been spelled phonetically. For example: *Dad said we awt to leave early.* Children rewrite the sentences correctly.
- Provide children with a blank crossword grid. Underneath the grid, they create their own clues (across and down) for words containing 'ie' and 'ei'.
- Do a spelling test for a selection of words spelled with 'ie' and 'ei'.

✈ Review

- Support children who are struggling to spell words containing silent letters by encouraging them to learn the words by pronouncing the silent letter. For example: *Wed – nes – day.*
- Ask children to point out and pronounce words with the letter string 'ough' that they come across in guided reading.
- Check that children understand and observe the spelling rule for 'ie' and 'ei' and know how to spell words that are exceptions.
- Include words with silent letters, the letter string 'ough' and 'ie'/'ei' spelling in regular spelling tests.

✈ Watch and listen

- Watch for children who are aware of tricky words that effectively lose a syllable in pronunciation such as *parliament, definite.*

TEST LINKS:

Section 1,
Spelling: Q3, 5, 15, 18, 19
Section 3,
Spelling: Q4, 8, 14, 18

WORKBOOK LINKS:

Pages 50–53

Noun classification

Write the words in the box below into the correct column in the table.

group	wealth	class	dog	school
city	London	mountain	disgust	practice
Mount Everest	health	desperation	grace	story
cousin	Mum	afternoon	Sunday	mirror
	St Thomas' Hospital		spite	

Common nouns	Proper nouns

Pronouns and determiners

Rewrite these sentences, replacing the repeated nouns with appropriate pronouns.

1. Stefan and Audrey stirred the cake mixture. Then, Stefan and Audrey put the cake mixture in a tin.

_____

2. The cat and the dog played for hours with the ball until finally the cat and the dog burst the ball.

_____

3. Mum and I bought some books but stupidly Mum and I left the books in the shop.

_____

Find as many examples as possible of pronouns, possessive pronouns, determiners, possessive determiners and demonstrative determiners in the passage below. Use a colour code to highlight each type.

Colour code

pronouns: [   ]

possessive pronouns: [   ]

determiners: [   ]

possessive determiners: [   ]

demonstrative determiners: [   ]

We went to see our grandparents last week. They live in an old, ramshackle cottage by the sea. On the first day, Dad and I ran up and down the sand dunes.

"Those are the same sand dunes I used to play on when I was a little boy," said Dad.

Grandma made the most amazing picnic which we ate on the beach.

"My mum makes the best cake!" said Dad.

"Yes, it's much better than mine," said Mum, winking at me.

Degrees of possibility

Write the modal verbs and adverbs that belong under each heading.

Uncertain	Possible	Probable	Certain

Conjunction word cards

Cut out the words below into separate word cards.

Working in pairs, take it in turns to choose a card and make up a sentence using the conjunction.

✂

unless	although	because
even though	after	since
whenever	before	as
once	while	if

Who, whom, whose?

Cut out the words below into separate word cards.

Working in pairs, take it in turns to choose a card and make up a sentence using the relative pronoun.

✂

who	**whom**	**whose**
which	**that**	

Tell me more!

Rewrite these sentences by expanding each noun phrase.

1. The dog slept on a bed in the corner of the barn.

_____

_____

_____

2. Our brother annoyed our neighbour by trampling on his flowers.

_____

_____

_____

3. The house by the lake was battered in the storm.

_____

_____

_____

4. Two singers from school were chosen to perform at the concert.

_____

_____

_____

From active to passive

Highlight the subject and object in each sentence below.

Now rewrite each sentence in the passive voice.

1. Mum arranged the flowers in a vase.

_____

_____

_____

2. The dentist expertly extracted my brother's tooth.

_____

_____

_____

3. Our head teacher warmly welcomed the visitor to our assembly.

_____

_____

_____

4. My best friend brought me to first-aid after I fell off the climbing frame.

_____

_____

_____

Cut out each sentence below into three separate strips.

Then cut out the punctuation marks.

Shuffle the strips of paper and put each sentence in the correct order, inserting the missing punctuation to indicate parenthesis.

| Our neighbours |
| the ones who breed pedigree dogs |
| are emigrating to Australia next year. |

| The problem with Gemma is |
| I've said this many times |
| she doesn't listen! |

| Prince Harry |
| the son of Prince Charles |
| raises money for a range of charities. |

| (|) | – | – | , | , |

What does it mean?

The words in the table below can start with either the prefix **re-** (with hyphen) or **re** (no hyphen). Use a dictionary to write a definition for each word.

Word	Definition	Word	Definition
re-sign		resign	
re-serve		reserve	
re-sort		resort	

Missing apostrophes

In this passage of text, no apostrophes have been used in contractions. Highlight the relevant words, then re-write the passage correctly on the lines below.

Weve been waiting for ages for the band to come on stage but finally that moments arrived! Theyve promised us a night to remember so well just have to wait and see. Ive been a big fan for years and Im just hoping they dont disappoint. Its going to be the most exciting night of my life!

_____

_____

_____

_____

_____

_____

_____

_____

_____

_____

_____

_____

_____

It's mine!

Turn the words displayed in the first and second columns in the tables below into phrases (or expanded noun phrases) to show possession.

Singular 'owner'	Noun	Phrase
my grandpa	scarf	
James	books	
the prince	sword	
our tortoise	shell	
the radio	aerial	
our class	furniture	

Plural 'owner'	Noun	Phrase
the princesses	crowns	
the children	Christmas presents	
the men	changing rooms	
our parents	wedding anniversary	
those ladies	dresses	
the trees	leaves	

Opposite meanings

Each of the prefixes in the box below can be added to the words listed in the table to form their opposite meanings. Choose the correct prefix and write the new word in the space provided.

mis il dis un ir in im

understand		practical	
decided		active	
arm		literate	
bearable		explicable	
apprehension		realistic	
regular		credit	
logical		belief	
connect		replaceable	
perfect		mature	

Which suffix?

Use appropriate suffixes to change each verb listed below into a noun; then change each noun into an adjective.

Verb	Noun	Adjective
vacate		
adore		
accept		
apply		
inform		
energise		

Use appropriate suffixes to change each adjective listed below into a noun.

Adjective	Noun	Adjective	Noun
electric		naughty	
lazy		rare	
public		brutal	
absurd		honest	

That doesn't sound right!

In the following passage of text, the words underlined and in bold do not make sense in the context of the sentence. Write the most suitable antonym above each one.

‾‾‾‾‾‾‾‾‾‾‾‾‾‾‾‾
↑

My <u>dreadful</u> day

‾‾‾‾‾‾‾‾‾‾‾‾‾‾‾‾
↑

My school report was very **<u>negative</u>**; Mum and Dad were so pleased that they took me out

‾‾‾‾‾‾‾‾‾‾‾‾‾‾‾‾
↑

for lunch to celebrate. The meal we had was so **<u>diabolical</u>** that Dad felt compelled to leave

‾‾‾‾‾‾‾‾‾‾‾‾‾‾‾‾
↑

a good tip. Afterwards, as the weather was so **<u>appalling</u>**, we went for a walk in the sunshine

‾‾‾‾‾‾‾‾‾‾‾‾‾‾‾‾
↑

and were delighted at the sight of the **<u>disgusting</u>** views of the countryside.

Sounds the same

Complete the grid below by writing the homophones (or near-homophones) as well as the definitions of the words listed in the first column.

Word	Definition	Homophone/ near-homophone	Definition
principle			
queue			
assent			
advice			
effect			
serial			
birth			
due			

Writing activity 1

Grammatical terms/word classes

Write a short descriptive paragraph about a mysterious person you come across while walking on the beach on a cold, winter's day.

Include a range of exciting adjectives, adverbs and verbs. Consider fronted adverbials to make your sentences more interesting and a range of sentence lengths. When you have finished, read back over your writing to check for sense and find ways of making it even better.

Writing activity 2

Functions of sentences

Commands

Write a set of instructions for looking after an imaginary creature. Ensure you use command (or imperative) verbs and adverbials of time. For example: *After that,* _____

Statements

Write six statements about tornadoes using facts that you have found on the internet or in library books.

Questions

What six questions would you ask your favourite celebrity or sportsperson if you interviewed them?

After each task above, check you have made your writing as interesting as possible and that you have used accurate punctuation.

Writing activity 3

Combining words, phrases and clauses

Write a passage about an activity you have done recently. Include expanded noun phrases and subordinate clauses in your sentences. Use co-ordinating conjunctions to link phrases and clauses too.

When you have finished, read back over your writing to check for sense and find ways of making it even better. Remember, expanded noun phrases do not just have to have one adjective qualifying a noun. For example: *As I paddled the canoe towards the shore, <u>the smiling instructor with the red, curly hair</u> came to help me.*

Writing activity 4

Forms, tense and consistency

Write a short story where you start in the present tense but 'flashback' to a time in the past. Include not only simple present and past tenses but also present and past progressive and present and past perfect to make your writing more interesting.

Check your writing when you have finished to make sure you have been consistent in your use of tenses. Do not forget to include all the other features of writing that can be used for dramatic effect, such as vivid description, imagery, a range of sentence lengths and starters, and direct speech.

Writing activity 5

Punctuation

Write a short passage which includes a dialogue between two people. It might be that one person is asking for help because they have got lost. What might they say to one another? Remember the rules of punctuation in direct speech.

In all your writing, make a conscious effort to check for punctuation errors as you self-edit. Consider how you can make your punctuation more varied – for example, replace a full stop with a semi-colon to join two closely related main clauses (remembering that the second clause does not now need to start with a capital letter).

Writing activity 6

Formal/informal speech and writing/subjunctive mood

Imagine you have an audience with the Prime Minister. Write a formal speech telling him/her that you represent a group of children who are protesting about wearing school uniform. Use your powers of persuasion, as well as formal vocabulary which should include the subjunctive mood, such as: *If I were in your position of power, I would not hesitate to change the law to enable individual schools to make their own decisions.*

Remember to include persuasive devices such as:

- emotive language

- rhetorical questions

- flattery

- facts, figures and statistics (you can make them up!)

- repetition.

GRAMMAR
PUNCTUATION & SPELLING

SATs CHALLENGE

YEAR 6

Workbook

FOR CHILDREN WORKING AT GREATER DEPTH

Scholastic Education, an imprint of Scholastic Ltd

Book End, Range Road, Witney, Oxfordshire, OX29 0YD

Registered office: Westfield Road, Southam, Warwickshire CV47 0RA

www.scholastic.co.uk

© 2018, Scholastic Ltd

1 2 3 4 5 6 7 8 9   8 9 0 1 2 3 4 5 6 7

British Library Cataloguing-in-Publication Data

A catalogue record for this book is available from the British Library.

ISBN 978-1407-17651-2

Printed and bound by Ashford Colour Press

Due to the nature of the web we cannot guarantee the content or links of any site mentioned. We strongly recommend that teachers check websites before using them in the classroom.

Every effort has been made to trace copyright holders for the works reproduced in this book, and the publishers apologise for any inadvertent omissions.

Extracts from National Curriculum for England, English Programme of Study © Crown Copyright. Reproduced under the terms of the Open Government Licence (OGL). www.nationalarchives.gov.uk/doc/open-government-licence/version/3/

Author Shelley Welsh

Editorial Rachel Morgan, Audrey Stokes, Shannon Keenlyside, Margaret Eaton

Cover and Series Design Neil Salt and Nicolle Thomas

Layout Alice Duggan

Illustrations Jennifer Naalchigar/The Bright Agency

Contents

How to use this book

This *Workbook* helps you to check what you already know, practise what you've learned and challenge yourself to fly higher!

You can work through all of the activities in order or you can dip in and out to brush up your skills or explore in more depth. Use the progress chart opposite to record which skills you've checked and practised. Aim higher by having a go at the questions in the *Skills Test Papers*.

You can check the answers at the back of the book.

What you should be able to do after you complete the skills check and practice questions. You can tick off each one as you can do it.

The title of the topic.

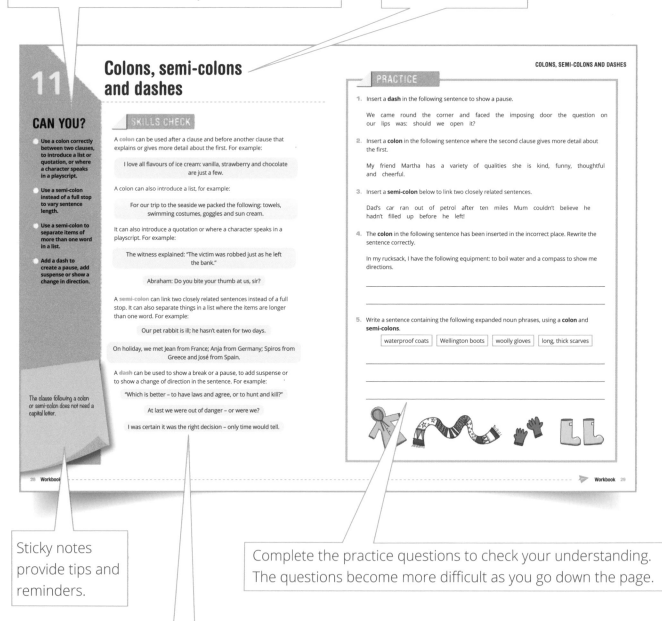

Sticky notes provide tips and reminders.

Complete the practice questions to check your understanding. The questions become more difficult as you go down the page.

Background information on the topic to help you answer the questions.

▼ Progress chart

Topic	Skills checked	Practised	Aimed higher
Word classes			
Pronouns and determiners			
Modal verbs and adverbs			
Sentence types			
Conjunctions and subordinate clauses			
Relative clauses			
Expanded noun phrases			
Verb tenses			
Passive verbs			
Brackets, dashes and commas			
Colons, semi-colons and dashes			
Hyphens and commas to avoid ambiguity			
Apostrophes to show contraction			
Apostrophes for possession			
Inverted commas			
Prefixes			
Suffixes			
Synonyms and antonyms			
Formal speech and writing			
Homophones and near-homophones			
Etymology and morphology			
Tricky spellings			

1

Word classes

- **Explain what a noun, an adjective, a verb and an adverb are.**

- **Identify common, proper and abstract nouns.**

- **Punctuate sentences starting with an adverb or an adverbial phrase correctly.**

- **Use adverbs to modify adjectives.**

Abstract noun

This type of common noun names things that cannot be seen, like emotions.

For example: As **fear** took hold of Vishwa, he was unable to move.

SKILLS CHECK

Nouns are naming words for people, animals, places and things. There are two different types of noun: **common nouns** and **proper nouns**. Common nouns name general things. Proper nouns name specific things and start with a capital.

A noun can be modified by an **adjective**.

> The **exceptional** courage of the soldiers helped win the war.

Verbs are 'doing' or 'being' words. They can be modified by **adverbs**. Adverbs can modify verbs by telling you more about manner (*calmly*), place (*there*), time (*today*) or degree (*very*).

> Chloe shivered **violently** because she had forgotten her coat.

An adverb can also say more about an adjective...

> It was a **ridiculously** expensive car.

...or more about another adverb.

> Sam ran **really** quickly to the front of the line.

An **adverbial** is a word or phrase that behaves like an adverb. If it comes at the start of a sentence, it is called a **fronted adverbial** and is followed by a **comma**.

> **After a long wait**, Frankie finally entered the enormous stadium to watch his favourite team.

Look at the different **word classes** in the sentence below.

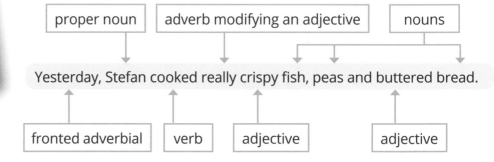

PRACTICE

1. Underline all the **nouns** in the sentences below.

   a. We walked to the shops but took the bus back.

   b. Our class visited the museum yesterday.

2. Underline the **adverb** that describes the **adjective** in this sentence.

   My really annoying sister is in trouble again.

3. Underline all the **verbs** in each sentence below.

   a. We practised our song until we were perfect.

   b. On Saturdays, Mia goes to the library and chooses a book.

4. Rewrite each sentence so that it starts with the **adverbial**. Remember to punctuate your sentences correctly.

   a. I look forward to a hot soak in the bath after a long day.

   _____

   _____

   b. The sailors spotted a pirate ship in the far distance.

   _____

   _____

5. a. Write a sentence using the word <u>light</u> as a **noun**.

   _____

   b. Write a sentence using the word <u>light</u> as a **verb**.

   _____

Pronouns and determiners

CAN YOU?

● Say what a pronoun and a possessive pronoun are, and give examples.

● Use pronouns in your writing.

● Say what a determiner is and give examples.

● Say what a possessive determiner and a demonstrative determiner are and give examples.

SKILLS CHECK

A **pronoun** can replace a noun to avoid repetition.

> Fred raised £50 doing a sponsored swim. **He** is planning to do **it** again next year.

Possessive pronouns show who owns something. They are used to replace the person doing the possessing and the item they possess.

> That bike is Grace's bike. ⟶ It's **hers**.

A **determiner** introduces a noun; it goes before any modifiers such as adjectives or other nouns. *The* is used to specify a 'known' noun; *a* and *an* are used to specify an 'unknown' noun. Use *an* before a word beginning with a vowel.

> the apple ⟶ the red apple   an apple ⟶ a red apple

A **possessive determiner** comes before a noun and shows that someone owns the noun. It replaces the possessor but not the item possessed.

> Mum took **her** books back to the library.

Some **demonstrative determiners** indicate the location of something; others show amounts.

> **Those** shoes are full price but there are **lots of** bargains over there.

PRACTICE

1. What nouns do the **pronouns** in bold refer to in the following sentence?

   Megan had never seen such a wonderful scooter; **it** was bright red with white handles and **she** couldn't believe it was hers.

   a. **it** refers to _____

   b. **she** refers to _____

2. Underline the **possessive pronouns** in the following sentence.

   That's not my coat, it's yours. Mine looks similar but I know yours has a missing button.

3. Replace the underlined nouns with **pronouns** and rewrite the sentence.

   <u>Mia and Kate</u> comforted <u>Mrs Smith</u> when <u>Mrs Smith</u> fell.

   _____

4. Complete the sentences using the **pronouns** <u>I</u> or <u>me</u>.

   a. Mum cooked Amelia and _____ a big breakfast.

   b. Flo and _____ had a picnic in the park.

   c. Dad and _____ worked in the garden all day.

5. Circle all the **determiners** in the sentence below.

   We had a last attempt at scoring a goal but the other team proved too strong for us.

6. Insert suitable **demonstrative determiners** in the sentence below.

   _____ children have dropped _____ litter so let's tell them to

   pick it up and put it in _____ bins.

7. Underline the **possessive determiners** in each sentence below.

   a. Archie passed the butter to his brother so he could butter his toast.

   b. Our grandparents like to travel to the seaside for their holidays.

   c. The boys picked up their books and put them back in their trays.

Modal verbs and adverbs

CAN YOU?

- Give examples of different modal verbs.

- Give examples of different adverbs that express certainty and possibility.

- Estimate the certainty of something expressed by modal verbs or adverbs.

- Use suitable modal verbs or adverbs to make your writing more precise.

SKILLS CHECK

A **modal verb** can change the meaning of the verb that follows it. It can indicate:

- **degrees of possibility**, for example:

  It **might** snow later on.

  Mum **will** pick us up at 7 o'clock.

- **obligation**, for example:

  I **ought to** practise my times tables.

- **ability**, for example:

  Gregor **can** say the alphabet backwards.

Some **adverbs** can also be used to show how likely or unlikely something is.

Maybe it will snow later on.

Modal verbs indicating degrees of possibility, ability and obligation	Adverbs indicating degrees of possibility
can	definitely
will	certainly
shall	possibly
must	surely
could	likely
would	unlikely
should	maybe
may	perhaps
might	
ought to	

PRACTICE

1. Underline the **modal verb** in each sentence below.

   a. We might go swimming tonight.

   b. You should help your mum by tidying your room.

2. Which sentence below uses a **modal verb** to indicate ability?

   Tick **one**.

   I might come to your house later.   ☐

   Henry can speak two languages.   ☐

   You should bring your umbrella in case it rains.   ☐

3. Underline the **adverb** in the sentence below that shows uncertainty.

   Sadly, we think it is unlikely that our hockey team will win the final.

4. Which sentence below uses an **adverb** to indicate certainty?

   Tick **one**.

   There are possibly two new pupils starting this term.   ☐

   We're definitely going to Scotland on holiday.   ☐

   Mum said that maybe she will take us to the cinema.   ☐

   Perhaps we need to put our coats on.   ☐

5. Write two sentences containing **adverbs** to indicate possibility and/or certainty, saying what you would do if you won £100.

   1. _____

   _____

   2. _____

   _____

4 Sentence types

CAN YOU?

- Explain what a statement, question, command and exclamation are.

- Punctuate statements, questions, commands and exclamations correctly.

SKILLS CHECK

	What is it?	Punctuation	Example
Statement	A **statement** is a sentence that tells you something.	Ends with a full stop.	*We are going away at Easter.*
Question	A **question** is a sentence that asks something. Sometimes, a question can be a statement followed by a comma and a **question tag**.	Ends with a question mark.	*Are you going away at Easter?* *You're going away at Easter, aren't you?*
Command	A **command** is a sentence that tells you to do something. It contains a command verb, often at the beginning of the sentence.	Ends with either a full stop or an exclamation mark.	*Finish your breakfast or we'll be late.*
Exclamation	An **exclamation** is a sentence where surprise, shock, pain or a strong emotion is expressed. It starts with *How* or *What* and contains a subject and verb.	Ends with an exclamation mark.	*How lovely it is to see you!*

PRACTICE

1. Tick the sentence below that is a **statement**.

   Tick **one**.

   You're coming to my house later, aren't you? ☐

   Mum is cooking spaghetti for our tea. ☐

   Don't be late as I want to play Monopoly. ☐

2. Write a **question** that would match this answer.

   Insects have six legs.

   _____

Exclamation marks

Can be used at the end of a command as well as at the end of an exclamation.

For example: Come back!

3. The punctuation is missing in the sentences below. Tick one box in each row to indicate the **sentence type**.

Sentence	Statement	Question	Command	Exclamation
What time does the film start				
What an amazing display of flowers that is				
We are meeting Sam and Joe at the shops				
Mix all the ingredients together				

4. Which sentence below is **punctuated** correctly?

Tick **one**.

Please tell me how old you are? ☐

Dan has a younger sister and an older brother, doesn't he? ☐

How wonderful that you are going to Australia? ☐

5. *What a surprise!*

a. Why is this not an **exclamation** sentence?

_____

b. Rewrite it so that it *is* an exclamation sentence.

_____

6. Write an example of each of the following **sentence** types.

Sentence type	Sentence
exclamation	
question (using a question tag)	
statement	
command	

5

Conjunctions and subordinate clauses

- Use co-ordinating conjunctions to link two words, phrases or clauses of equal importance.

- Use subordinating conjunctions to introduce subordinate clauses.

- Explain what a subordinate clause and a main clause are.

- Use a range of conjunctions in your writing.

SKILLS CHECK

A **co-ordinating conjunction** links two words, phrases or clauses of equal importance. These are:

| and | nor | but | or | yet | so |

> Sami likes vegetables **but** he's not keen on fruit.

A **subordinate clause** is introduced by a **subordinating conjunction**. For example:

| however | although | while | as | because | unless |

A subordinate clause does not make sense on its own – it is not a complete sentence. For example:

> Our teacher said we would miss our break **unless we behaved**.

"Our teacher said we would miss our break" is the **main clause** – it makes sense on its own.

Clauses

Contain a subject and a verb. They are a complete sentences on their own.

PRACTICE

1. Tick **one** box in each row to show whether the clauses in bold are **main clauses** or **subordinate clauses**.

Sentence	Main clause	Subordinate clause
Even though she had eaten all her lunch, **Sophie was still hungry**.		
Bethan went to the dentist **after Mum picked her up from school**.		
As you have been talking all morning, you probably didn't hear my instructions.		
It was clear that Maggie had practised her spellings since she got every single one correct.		

2. Complete the following sentences using appropriate **conjunctions** from the box. Use each conjunction only once.

| and | but | so |

It started to rain _____ we packed our waterproofs _____ wellies. I asked

if we should bring umbrellas _____ Mum said no.

3. Underline the **conjunction** in each sentence below.

   a. Don't stand up until the train has stopped.

   b. Paula didn't know her 9-times tables or her 12-times tables.

4. Complete the following sentence by adding a suitable **main clause** in front of the **subordinate clause**.

_____ although she was only 11 years old.

5. Rewrite the following sentence so that it starts with the **subordinate clause**. Remember to punctuate your sentence correctly.

Stella was stung by a wasp while she was helping Dad in the garden.

_____

6. Explain why the clause in bold below is not a **main clause**.

Erin spent the day indoors **because she had a bad cold**.

_____

6 Relative clauses

CAN YOU?

- Describe what a relative clause is.

- Give examples of relative pronouns that introduce a relative clause.

- Identify and use relative clauses where the relative pronoun has been omitted.

SKILLS CHECK

A **relative clause** is a type of subordinate clause. It is normally introduced by a **relative pronoun**.

who	that	which	whose	whom

Relative clauses can also begin with the adverbs *when* and *where*. They are used to define the noun that comes before them.

> The people **who explored the world hundreds of years ago** didn't have maps.

The relative pronoun *whom* is used as the object of the verb. It is not often used and is considered quite formal. For example:

> The new pupils **whom** you met yesterday are excited about joining our school.

Sometimes, the relative pronoun is implied. For example:

> The rain gauge we made showed 3cm of rain this morning.

> The rain gauge **that** we made showed 3cm of rain this morning.

PRACTICE

1. Underline the **relative clause** in each sentence below.

   a. The head teacher who visited from the neighbouring school was impressed with our work.

   b. The boy whose shoes had been found in lost property was embarrassed.

   c. Otters are playful creatures which live in clean rivers.

   d. We saw layers of sedimentary rock that were folded and twisted.

2. Which option completes the sentence below?

The soldiers, _____ courage had helped win the war, are remembered every year.

Tick **one**.

who ☐   which ☐   whose ☐   that ☐

3. Insert a suitable **relative pronoun** in the sentences below.

a. The investigation, _____ we started before break, took much longer than we thought.

b. My uncle, _____ works for the local council, says pollution is a huge problem.

c. Our neighbour, _____ car was stolen last week, has had to get the bus to work.

d. The day _____ I was born is famous for many other reasons!

4. Tick the sentence where the **relative pronoun** cannot be omitted.

Tick **one**.

The goldfish which we won at the local fair
is still alive and splashing.   ☐

Our local restaurant, whose owners are from
Spain, is closing next week.   ☐

The house which Gina's parents have just
bought is in a small, country village.   ☐

That car that you bought is amazing!   ☐

5. Insert suitable **relative pronouns** in the passage below.

The boy to _____ you were just talking is my cousin. His name is Sean _____ is Irish.

The town _____ he lives is just outside Dublin.

7 Expanded noun phrases

CAN YOU?

- Explain what a noun phrase is.

- Explain how to make an expanded noun phrase.

- Identify an expanded noun phrase in a sentence.

- Use a range of expanded noun phrases in your writing.

SKILLS CHECK

A **noun phrase** is a phrase that is about a **noun**. For example:

> **Those books** are mine.

> Have you got **any money**?

> Mum gave me **a biscuit**.

You can **expand** a noun phrase to give extra detail about the noun. The noun might be modified by an **adjective**, another **noun** and/or a **preposition phrase**. For example:

> **Those scary books** are mine.

> I like **your football shirt**.

> How much is **that dog in the window**?

> **Modify**
>
> Means to make minor changes to something, usually to improve it.

PRACTICE

1. Underline the **noun phrase** in each sentence below.

   a. We bought some apples.

   b. Dad baked a cake.

   c. Our dog is hungry.

   d. Please wash the dishes.

2. Underline the **expanded noun phrase** in each sentence below.

   a. Finally, we arrived at the quaint seaside town.

   b. Out of the blue, a mysterious stranger in a dark cloak stepped in front of us.

   c. Mrs Wilkinson wore a vibrant yellow hat with a bunch of red cherries on the side.

   d. The wolf with the sharp, white fangs jumped off the rocks.

3. Underline the longest possible **expanded noun phrase** in the sentence below.

   She is a determined, well-respected athlete who has represented her country in

   international competitions.

4. Modify the **noun phrases** on the left to turn them into **expanded noun phrases**.

Noun phrase	Expanded noun phrase
some sharks	
a lot of people	
the forest	
two teachers	

5. Now use the **expanded noun phrases** that you created in question 4 to write your own sentences on the lines below.

   a. _____

   b. _____

   c. _____

   d. _____

Verb tenses

● **Identify verbs in the simple past and present tenses, the past and present progressive tenses and the past and present perfect tenses.**

● **Use a variety of verb tenses depending on the context of your writing.**

● **Explain when to use the different tenses.**

SKILLS CHECK

We use a range of different **tenses** in our speech and writing to show when and how something happens or is happening.

Tense	What it does and how it is formed	Examples
simple present	Describes an action that is happening now or is often repeated. States a fact or opinion.	*I **walk** to school every Monday.* *We **eat** breakfast in the mornings at 8 o'clock.* *The Sahara **engulfs** most of North Africa.* *You **watch** too much television.*
present progressive	Describes an action happening now. Formed by the present tense of 'to be' and the present participle of the verb.	*I **am eating** my lunch now.* *They **are sleeping** in the tent.*
simple past	Describes something that has happened in the past and is completed.	*She **spoke** in assembly yesterday.* *We **wrote** a story for homework.*
past progressive	Highlights the clause which tells you at what point in the past the action was in progress. Formed by the simple past tense of 'to be' and the present participle of the verb.	*Tom **was running** towards the ice-cream van when it drove away.* *As they **were snoring** all night, we couldn't get any sleep.*
present perfect	Describes an action that started in the past and continues in the present. Also, describes something that happened in the past but is important at the time of speaking. Formed by the present tense of 'to have' and the past participle of the verb.	*I **have lived** in Manchester all my life.* *We **have listened** to your instructions carefully and we are now ready to climb the mountain.*
past perfect	Describes an action completed in the past before something else happened. Formed by the past tense of 'to have' and the past participle of the verb.	*I **had** just **eaten** my breakfast when the doorbell rang.* *We **had spent** a lovely day on the beach when it suddenly began to rain.*

PRACTICE

1. Rewrite these sentences so that they are in the **simple present tense**.

   a. I brushed my teeth before I went to bed.

   _____

   b. After I scored a goal, I couldn't stop smiling.

   _____

2. Which sentence below uses the **past perfect form**?

   Tick **one**.

   Mum has been to Buckingham Palace but she didn't see the Queen. ☐

   Dad had just woken up when the phone began to ring. ☐

   We were planning a picnic in the park when it started to rain. ☐

   Everyone in our class signed a birthday card for our teacher. ☐

3. Complete the sentences below using the **simple past tense** of the verbs in the boxes.

   Our class _____ on a trip to the museum. We _____ some Egyptian

   | go |

   | see |

   artefacts and _____ some hieroglyphic texts.

   | read |

4. Underline the verbs in the **present progressive tense** in the sentences below.

   a. We are making models of the Globe Theatre which we will display in the hall.

   b. Sian is jumping on the trampoline even though she has been told not to.

   c. Those dogs are running wild all over the park which is annoying.

   d. My sister is crying because Mum won't let her stay up late.

5. Which sentence below uses the **present perfect form**?

Tick **one**.

We thought we had reached the end of the path but there was still a long way to go. ☐

Have you seen my new pencil case? ☐

Moira and Chloe have curly, red hair. ☐

The whole class is going to watch the handball game. ☐

6. Rewrite these sentences so that the verbs in bold are in the **past progressive tense**.

a. Alfie **mumbled** that he didn't like sprouts or peas.

_____

b. We called Samir but he **went** in the opposite direction.

_____

c. While we **strolled** along the canal, we saw a shoal of fish and some ducks.

_____

7. Complete the sentences below using the **present perfect tense** of the verbs in the boxes.

My parents _____ about moving house.

be

They _____ a cottage in the countryside which I think they

view

_____ in love with.

fall

8. Tick the sentence that uses **verb tenses** correctly.

Tick **one**.

My best friend was been teased about his new haircut. ☐

When I was young, I am always being naughty. ☐

In our class, there is one girl from Poland and there are two boys from India. ☐

Yesterday, we have thought of ways to help our teacher. ☐

9. Write **four** sentences about what you did last weekend, using both the **simple past** and the **past progressive tense**. Use a range of sentence starters and conjunctions.

1. _____

_____

2. _____

_____

3. _____

_____

4. _____

_____

9 Passive verbs

CAN YOU?

- Say whether a sentence is written in the active voice or the passive voice.

- Change a sentence written in the active voice to the passive voice and vice versa.

- Identify the subject and object in a sentence.

SKILLS CHECK

We mostly write in the **active voice**. In a sentence written in the active voice, the **subject** is 'doing' or 'being' something. If there is an **object**, it is what the subject is 'acting upon'. For example:

A tall, hunched, old man | opened | the creaking door.

subject (expanded noun phrase) | verb | object (expanded noun phrase)

In **passive-voice** sentences, the noun, proper noun, pronoun or noun phrase that would be the object in an active-voice sentence becomes the subject; this subject undergoes the action, rather than doing it. For example:

The creaking door | was opened | by a tall, hunched, old man.

subject (expanded noun phrase) | verb | prepositional phrase/agent

The subject from the original active-voice sentence becomes part of a **prepositional phrase** and is called the **agent**. It isn't always included. For example:

The creaking door was opened.

The **passive verb** is formed by combining the verb 'to be' with the **past participle** of the main verb.

The passive voice is often used in formal writing or where the action or situation is more important than who or what did or caused it.

PRACTICE

1. Tick **one** box in each row to show whether each sentence is in the **active voice** or the **passive voice**.

Sentence	Active voice	Passive voice
Mum and Dad cheered me when I scored the winning goal.		
The last piece of cake was eaten by my greedy little brother!		
Flo and Max found fossils in the rocks by the edge of the sea.		
The messy art area was tidied by Scarlet.		

2. Underline the **subject** and circle the **object** in each of these active-voice sentences. Then rewrite each sentence in the **passive voice**.

   a. Animal-loving volunteers care for the abandoned pets.

   _____

   b. Anya and Abigail won the singing competition.

   _____

   c. The head teacher introduced the visiting author.

   _____

3. Rewrite the sentence below so that it is in the **active voice**.

   The trophy was presented by a local sports personality.

   _____

4. a. Write a sentence in the **passive voice** which includes the **agent**.

   _____

   b. Write a sentence in the **passive voice** which does **not** include the **agent**.

   _____

10

Brackets, dashes and commas

CAN YOU?

- Identify parenthesis in a sentence.

- Explain what parenthesis means.

- Use brackets, dashes and commas correctly to indicate parenthesis.

- Remember that the word, phrase or clause in parenthesis makes no sense on its/their own, and what is 'outside' the parenthesis makes sense as a main clause.

SKILLS CHECK

Parenthesis means inserting a word, phrase or clause as an explanation or afterthought into a sentence that would still make sense without it there.

Brackets, **dashes** and **commas** can be used to indicate parenthesis. They go around the words that sit inside them.

There are many reasons (and sadly I know from bitter experience) not to eat in that restaurant.

There are many reasons – and sadly I know from bitter experience – not to eat in that restaurant.

There are many reasons, and sadly I know from bitter experience, not to eat in that restaurant.

Dashes and commas can only come inside the sentence, whereas brackets can come either inside a sentence or around a word, phrase or clause at the end of a sentence.

PRACTICE

1. Tick the sentence below that uses **dashes** correctly to show parenthesis.

Tick **one**.

It took Lucas ages to answer the question – being exceptionally hard and everyone – breathed a sigh of relief. ☐

It took Lucas ages to answer – the question being exceptionally hard and everyone – breathed a sigh of relief. ☐

It took Lucas ages to answer – the question being exceptionally hard – and everyone breathed a sigh of relief. ☐

It took Lucas – ages to answer being exceptionally hard – and everyone breathed a sigh of relief. ☐

2. Insert a **pair of brackets** in the appropriate places in each sentence below to show parenthesis.

   a. My great-uncle who seems pretty ancient has just run a marathon.

   b. Chloe determined and focused summited the mountain in record time.

   c. The winning athletes none of whom seemed out of breath did a lap of honour.

   d. After an amazing birthday tea pizza, coleslaw, ice cream and fruit, I blew out the candles on my birthday cake.

3. Write three of your own sentences containing each of the following forms of punctuation to indicate parenthesis: **brackets, dashes** and **commas**.

   1. _____

   2. _____

   3. _____

4. Insert a **pair of brackets** in the appropriate places in each sentence below.

   a. It's always cold in Edinburgh in the winter though the Shetland Isles are colder still.

   b. Sam ordered a starter, main meal and a dessert despite just having had a sandwich.

   c. We loved the play despite the main actor forgetting some of his lines though only in the second act.

   d. Our teacher handed our tests back and I was thrilled with my mark 18 out of 20.

5. Insert a suitable word, phrase or clause in **parenthesis** in the gap in each sentence below. Use punctuation of your choice.

   a. The doctor _____ bandaged my arm expertly.

   b. Eating too much fried food _____ can lead to health problems.

   c. Our school library stocks many different genres _____ but my favourite books are mysteries.

11

Colons, semi-colons and dashes

- Use a colon correctly between two clauses, to introduce a list or quotation, or where a character speaks in a playscript.

- Use a semi-colon instead of a full stop to vary sentence length.

- Use a semi-colon to separate items of more than one word in a list.

- Add a dash to create a pause, add suspense or show a change in direction.

The clause following a colon or semi-colon does not need a capital letter.

SKILLS CHECK

A **colon** can be used after a clause and before another clause that explains or gives more detail about the first. For example:

> I love all flavours of ice cream: vanilla, strawberry and chocolate are just a few.

A colon can also introduce a list, for example:

> For our trip to the seaside we packed the following: towels, swimming costumes, goggles and sun cream.

It can also introduce a quotation or where a character speaks in a playscript. For example:

> The witness explained: "The victim was robbed just as he left the bank."

> Abraham: Do you bite your thumb at us, sir?

A **semi-colon** can link two closely related sentences instead of a full stop. It can also separate things in a list where the items are longer than one word. For example:

> Our pet rabbit is ill; he hasn't eaten for two days.

> On holiday, we met Jean from France; Anja from Germany; Spiros from Greece and José from Spain.

A **dash** can be used to show a break or a pause, to add suspense or to show a change of direction in the sentence. For example:

> "Which is better – to have laws and agree, or to hunt and kill?"

> At last we were out of danger – or were we?

> I was certain it was the right decision – only time would tell.

PRACTICE

1. Insert a **dash** in the following sentence to show a pause.

We came round the corner and faced the imposing door the question on our lips was: should we open it?

2. Insert a **colon** in the following sentence where the second clause gives more detail about the first.

My friend Martha has a variety of qualities she is kind, funny, thoughtful and cheerful.

3. Insert a **semi-colon** below to link two closely related sentences.

Dad's car ran out of petrol after ten miles Mum couldn't believe he hadn't filled up before he left!

4. The **colon** in the following sentence has been inserted in the incorrect place. Rewrite the sentence correctly.

In my rucksack, I have the following equipment: to boil water and a compass to show me directions.

_____

_____

5. Write a sentence containing the following expanded noun phrases, using a **colon** and **semi-colons**.

| waterproof coats | Wellington boots | woolly gloves | long, thick scarves |

_____

_____

_____

12

Hyphens and commas to avoid ambiguity

CAN YOU?

- Explain what ambiguity is.

- Explain the difference in meaning between a hyphenated and non-hyphenated word.

- Explain how the inclusion of a comma can affect the meaning of a sentence.

- Use hyphens and commas to avoid ambiguity.

SKILLS CHECK

We use the word **ambiguity** to say when a word or a group of words can have more than one meaning. This can happen if we do not punctuate correctly.

To avoid ambiguity, we can use **hyphens**:

- in **compound words**

  a high-speed motorbike

(not a high speed motorbike)

- to make a distinction between two words whose meaning could be ambiguous without it

  re-cover ⟶ to cover something again

  recover ⟶ to get well again or get back

We can also use **commas** to avoid ambiguity:

"Let's eat Granny," said the children.

"Let's eat, Granny," said the children.

PRACTICE

1. Explain the different **meanings** of the sentences below.

   a. The pupil thinks the teacher is improving in English.

   _____

   b. The pupil, thinks the teacher, is improving in English.

   _____

2. Show the difference in **meaning** of each pair of words in the box by writing a sentence using each one in context.

| a. re-sign   resign   b. re-form   reform   c. re-count   recount |

a. (i) _____

a. (ii) _____

b. (i) _____

b. (ii) _____

c. (i) _____

c. (ii) _____

3. Place a **hyphen** between two adjacent words in each sentence to form a **compound word** and so avoid ambiguity.

a. The Lord Mayor is a hard working man who rarely takes a holiday.

b. My auntie Cath is a silver service waitress in the best restaurant in town.

c. Our school librarian was wearing a light blue scarf.

4. a. Write a sentence where the omission of a **comma** (or **commas**) affects the meaning.

_____

b. Now write the same sentence, this time including a **comma** (or **commas**) to affect the meaning.

_____

13 Apostrophes to show contraction

CAN YOU?

- Use apostrophes to contract words.

- Explain what letter or letters have been replaced by the apostrophe.

- Write an apostrophe in the correct position and at the correct height.

- Write the full form of a word that has been contracted.

SKILLS CHECK

We can use an **apostrophe** to show where a letter (or letters) have been left out of a word.

we have ⟶ we've

There are some words that you just have to learn to spell.

will not ⟶ won't

It is important to orient and position the apostrophe precisely. Remember, it is shaped like a comma but sits at the same height as inverted commas. It must be placed exactly where the omitted letter or letters would be.

"I've always liked a cup of tea in the mornings," said Mum.

PRACTICE

1. Write each **contracted** word in its full form.

   a. couldn't _____

   b. there's _____

   c. shan't _____

   d. they're _____

   e. wouldn't've _____

2. Write the two possible full forms of these **contractions**.

a. they'd _____   _____

b. I'd   _____   _____

c. he's   _____   _____

3. Which sentence uses **apostrophes** correctly?

Tick **one**.

Theres' no such thing as ghosts, we've been told. ☐

There's no such thing as ghosts, w'eve been told. ☐

Theres no such thing as ghost's, we've been told. ☐

There's no such thing as ghosts, we've been told. ☐

4. Write the **contracted** form for each pair or group of words.

Word pairs/groups of words	Contracted form	Word pairs/groups of words	Contracted form
you are		she has	
might not have		they are	
they had		Erin is	
can not		should not have	
Stanley has		is not	

14

Apostrophes for possession

- Use an apostrophe to indicate possession correctly.

- Say to whom an object belongs based on the word that has an apostrophe.

- Use an apostrophe to indicate possession in plural nouns correctly.

- Use an apostrophe after singular and plural nouns ending in double 's'.

SKILLS CHECK

Apostrophes can show that something belongs to someone. It is important to orient and position the apostrophe precisely. Remember, it is shaped like a comma but sits at the same height as inverted commas.

To show possession of a singular noun or proper noun, the apostrophe is positioned after the final letter of the noun, or proper noun followed by an **s**.

> Our neighbour's garden gate is open.

> Abi's book is on the table.

With irregular plurals, place the apostrophe after the final letter then add an **s**.

> The children's shoes are cluttering up the hall.

In plural nouns ending in **s**, add the apostrophe after the **s**.

> The doctors' working hours have been extended at my local surgery.

For proper nouns ending in **s**, the apostrophe comes after the final **s** and is followed by an extra **s**.

> James's tonsils have been hurting for days.

PRACTICE

1. Which sentence has been correctly punctuated with an **apostrophe**?

Tick **one**.

Mrs Smiths' lessons are always great fun. ☐

The boys' jumpers were found in lost property. ☐

Some childrens' parents help out at school. ☐

Our dads garden tool's are his pride and joy. ☐

2. Rewrite the following phrases using an **apostrophe** to indicate possession. The first one has been done for you.

Phrase	Phrase with apostrophe
the books belonging to James	James's books
the wedding day of our parents	
the crown belonging to the princess	
the horses belonging to the princes	

3. Rewrite the sentences below, inserting the missing **apostrophe** in each.

a. The mens toilets were closed for refurbishment.

_____

b. My parents celebrated their anniversary on my uncles boat.

_____

c. Our classs favourite subjects are art and geography.

_____

d. The dresses collars are white and pointy and the pockets are a contrasting colour.

_____

4. What is the rule for using an **apostrophe** to show possession in regular and irregular plural nouns?

_____

_____

15

Inverted commas

CAN YOU?

● Use inverted commas to punctuate direct speech.

● Position your inverted commas correctly.

● Remember to place closing inverted commas after the final punctuation mark of direct speech.

● Change reported speech to direct speech.

SKILLS CHECK

Inverted commas are used to show where spoken words start and finish in direct speech.

Opening inverted commas look like back-to-front and upside-down commas.

“

Closing inverted commas look like normal commas.

”

Closing inverted commas come after the final punctuation mark.

“We really must visit the countryside more often,” said Mum.

We can also use inverted commas for quotes and quotations.

The eyewitness reported that the thief drove off “in an old, silver Fiat.”

“But soft, what light through yonder window breaks?”

Inverted commas can be either single or double. Be consistent – don't mix the two types in your writing.

‘Come to my office at break time, please.’

“I'll pick you up at 5 o'clock.”

PRACTICE

1. Which sentence is correctly punctuated with **inverted commas**?

Tick **one**.

“How unbelievable that you are wearing the same dress as me!” exclaimed Mia. ☐

“How unbelievable that you are wearing the same dress as me”! exclaimed Mia. ☐

“How unbelievable that you are wearing the same dress as me, exclaimed Mia!” ☐

“How unbelievable that you are wearing the same dress as me! exclaimed” Mia. ☐

2. Insert the missing **inverted commas** and the **final punctuation mark** for any **direct speech** in the short passage below.

It's time to get in the car said Dad. Otherwise, we'll never get there

I ran down the stairs, grabbed my bag and jumped into the car.

Dad started the engine. Mum's going to make us late if she doesn't come soon he grumbled. Luckily, at that moment, Mum came out of the house, locked the door and got into the car.

Have you turned off the television asked Dad.

Oh no exclaimed Mum. I'm pretty sure I haven't

3. Rewrite the following sentences as **direct speech**, using correct punctuation and making any necessary changes to the sentence.

   a. The judge said he would announce the winner after lunch.

   _____

   b. If we didn't tidy our bedroom, we couldn't go to the park Mum said.

   _____

   c. Dad said he was very pleased with the work we had done in the garden.

   _____

4. Explain what is wrong with each of the following sentences. Write your answer on the line below each one.

   a. "I'm not sure I'll be able to come to your house later,' said Kris.

   _____

   b. "Surely you haven't finished your homework already"? asked Dad.

   _____

Prefixes

SKILLS CHECK

A **root** is part of a word to which a **prefix** can be added to make a new word from the same **word family**. Most prefixes are added to the start of the root word without changing the spelling.

> This is a regular hexagon.
>
> This is an **ir**regular hexagon.

The following prefixes have a negative meaning:

| un | dis | mis | il | ir | in | im |

However, **in** can also mean **in/into**.

The prefix **re** usually means to repeat or to do again. There can be different meanings, depending on whether it is hyphenated to the root word or not.

> Eamon make a mistake when signing the document so he had to **re-sign** it.

> After 20 years as president of the company, Erin **resigned** from her job to pursue her hobbies full time.

Some prefixes come from Greek and Latin.

Knowing the meaning of these will help you to know the meaning of some words and how to spell them in English.

PRACTICE

1. Select a **prefix** from the box to make a new word from each word below.

ir	un	il	mis	de	in

_____believable _____destructible _____inform

_____responsible _____compose _____logical

2. Write two words that you can make from the root **rupt** using **two different prefixes**.

1. _____ 2. _____

3. Write the meaning of the **prefix** in each word below. You can use a dictionary to help you.

Words	Prefix meaning
subway	
autobiography	
bisect	
monotone	
universal	

4. The following pairs of words have different meanings; one is hyphenated to the root word and one is not. Write a sentence for each to show the difference in meaning.

a. recover _____

_____

b. re-cover _____

_____

c. represent _____

_____

d. re-present _____

_____

Suffixes

CAN YOU?

- Change verbs into adjectives and adverbs by adding suffixes.

- Change verbs into nouns by adding suffixes.

- Change nouns into adjectives by adding suffixes.

- Add suffixes starting with a vowel to words ending in 'fer'.

SKILLS CHECK

A **suffix** is a letter or group of letters that can be added to the end of a word. Sometimes, adding a suffix will change the word class.

Verbs to adjectives	manage	manage**able**
	insist	insist**ent**
Verbs to nouns	realise	realisa**tion** / reali**ty**
	apply	applic**ant** / applic**ation**
Verbs to adverbs	notice	notice**ably**
	horrify	horrif**ically**
Nouns to adjectives	space	spa**cious**
	nutrition	nutri**tious**
	office	offi**cial** / offi**cious**
	essence	essen**tial**

When adding a suffix beginning with a vowel to a word ending in **fer**, you double the **r** if **fer** is still stressed when the suffix is added. If **fer** is not stressed, you do not double the **r**. For example:

refer → referred   refer → reference

PRACTICE

1. Add an appropriate **suffix**, **ed**, **ence** or **ing**, to each of the words below to make a new word. Then write a sentence using each word in context. Remember the spelling rule.

Word	Word + suffix	Sentence
differ		
transfer		
infer		

2. Add a suitable **suffix** to each verb below, then write the words in the correct column in the table. Use your dictionary to support you.

consider   adore   terrify   reside   depend

apply   prefer   vacate   correspond

Nouns	Adjectives

18 Synonyms and antonyms

CAN YOU?

- Explain what synonyms and antonyms are.

- Name a synonym for a given word.

- Name an antonym for a given word.

- Make an antonym by adding a negative prefix to a word.

Make sure the synonym you choose makes sense in the context of the sentence!

SKILLS CHECK

The word **synonym** is used to describe words that have the same, or very similar, meanings.

push ←→ shove

smile ←→ grin

The word **antonym** is used to describe words that are opposite in meaning.

weak → strong

Many antonyms are made by adding a **negative prefix** to the **root** word.

understand → misunderstand

agree → disagree

PRACTICE

1. Read this sentence: Timothy Wiggins likes to amble to the local shops every morning.

   Tick the word that is closest in meaning to *amble*.

   Tick **one**.

   run ☐   skip ☐   walk slowly ☐   rollerskate ☐

2. Tick the word that is an **antonym** for *frenzied*.

   Tick **one**.

   distraught ☐   calm ☐   uncontrolled ☐   frantic ☐

3. Which two words in the sentence below are **synonyms** of each other? Write them on the line below.

   The delighted king complimented the chivalrous knight on his courteous behaviour towards his haughty daughter.

   _____

4. Rewrite the sentence below, replacing the words in bold with suitable **synonyms**.

   Mr Harris, who is **industrious**, **trustworthy** and **obliging**, received a round of applause from the audience as he collected his award.

   _____

   _____

   _____

5. Add a **prefix** to each word to form its **antonym**.

   a. _____inform

   b. _____practical

   c. _____credible

   d. _____logical

19 Formal speech and writing

CAN YOU?

- Distinguish between formal and informal language.

- Use the subjunctive mood.

SKILLS CHECK

Informal speech and writing is a relaxed and chatty way of communicating that you would normally use with family and friends.

> "Hiya!"

Non-Standard English is when speech or writing is grammatically incorrect. It might be that the **subject** and **verb** don't agree.

> I done my homework.

For **formal speech and writing**, **Standard English** – which is grammatically correct – is used, as well as more formal vocabulary; it may also be in the **passive voice**.

> We have been invited to participate.

(Standard English, formal, passive voice)

> We've been asked to join in.

(Standard English, informal, passive voice)

The **subjunctive mood** can be used in formal speech and writing.

> If there **were** to be a fire, please proceed to the exits to the rear of the hall.

It can also be used to express a wish or an imaginary state.

> If only I **were** ten years younger!

PRACTICE

1. Rewrite each sentence below using **Standard English**.

   a. Shila ain't got no homework tonight.

   _____

   b. Give them books to me.

   _____

2. Tick the verb that would complete the sentence below so that it is in the **subjunctive mood**.

    If I _____ to train hard, I could make the Olympics one day!

    Tick **one**.

    could ☐   tried ☐   had ☐   were ☐

3. Draw lines to match each sentence below with its description on the right.

I am delighted to welcome our esteemed guest, Mr Joseph Bloggs.	No subject-verb agreement
It ain't half good to see you, Joe.	Formal speech
Was you surprised to see Joe here?	Non-Standard English
Here he is – welcome to the one and only Joseph Bloggs!	Informal speech

4. Rewrite the sentence below so that there is **subject-verb agreement**.

    We was at the cinema with our friends.

    _____

5. Which sentence is written in **Standard English**?

    Tick **one**.

    Beth seen that new TV programme last night. ☐

    We haven't seen our cousins for about a year. ☐

    You seen that film last week, didn't you? ☐

    They seen lots of different species of birds at the zoo. ☐

20 Homophones and near-homophones

CAN YOU?

- Explain what a homophone is.

- Give examples of homophones and their different meanings.

- Explain what a near-homophone is.

- Give examples of homophones and their different meanings.

Homophones are words that sound the same but have a different meaning and spelling.

bear/bare

Near-homophones are words that sound almost the same but have a different meaning and spelling.

quiet/quite

PRACTICE

1. Circle the correct **homophone** in each sentence below.

   a. Mike towed / toad the boat to the coast.

   b. The Three Wise Men arrived bearing / baring gifts.

   c. Mum's favourite cereal / serial is on TV tonight.

   d. The bridegroom walked down the aisle / isle with his bride.

2. Find the incorrect **homophone** in each sentence below. Write the correct word on the line below each sentence.

    a. I guest that our teacher was joking when he said there would be no homework.

    _____

    b. My younger sister began to whale when she was stung by a wasp.

    _____

    c. Our town was badly effected by the storm last night.

    _____

    d. The principle actor in the play has come down with a cold.

    _____

3. Write a rule to help you remember how to spell the following **homophones**.

    a. principal and principle

    _____

    b. affect and effect

    _____

    c. practice and practise

    _____

4. Write a **near-homophone** for each word on the left.

    advice   _____

    accept   _____

    wary   _____

    access   _____

21

Etymology and morphology

- Use your knowledge of etymology and morphology to help in spelling and understanding words.

SKILLS CHECK

A word's **etymology** is its origins in earlier forms of English or other languages, and how its form – **morphology** – and meaning have changed.

Much of our vocabulary has come from many different sources. English also borrows **prefixes** and **suffixes** from Greek and Latin. Understanding the meaning of these can help you work out the meaning of many words.

Prefix	Origin	Meaning	Example
aqua	Latin	water	aquamarine, aquarium
ambi	Latin	both	ambiguous, ambidextrous
hydra	Greek	water	hydrate, hydrant
geo	Greek	earth	geology, geography

PRACTICE

1. Write an English word derived from each Greek **prefix** on the left.

Greek prefix	Meaning	English word
agros	cultivated land	
gigas	enormous	
autos	self	
tele	far off	

2. What does the root **phon** mean in the **word family** below?

| telephone | phonics | symphony | phoneme |

Tick **one**.

sight ☐   musical ☐   sound ☐   far away ☐

3. Draw lines to match these Greek and Latin **prefixes** to their equivalent number.

| tri | | 6 |

| hex | | 10 |

| mono | | 3 |

| deca | | 1 |

4. Circle the word in each group below that does not belong in the **word family**.

a. finite   finish   infinity   final   fine

b. transport   transfer   tranquil   transit   transatlantic

5. Complete the table by writing an English word formed from each Latin word.

Latin	Definition	English word
cent	hundred	
alter	change	
spectare	watch	
audire	hear	

6. a. Write three words that you can make using the root **vis**.

_____

_____

_____

b. What does the root **vis** mean? _____

22

Tricky spellings

CAN YOU?

- Spell words with silent letters correctly.

- Spell words containing 'ough' correctly.

- Spell words with the /ee/ sound spelled 'ie'.

- Spell words with the /ee/ sound spelled 'ei' after 'c'.

- Spell words that are exceptions to the rule.

SKILLS CHECK

Some words in English are tricky to spell for different reasons; they may contain **silent letters** or **letter strings**, such as **ough**, that are pronounced differently depending on the word. Some rules, such as spelling the **/ee/** sound **ei** after **c**, have many exceptions.

Silent letters

Silent letter	Examples
k is always at the beginning of a word and is followed by an **n**	**k**now
g is followed by an **n**	**g**nat
h goes with other letters, especially **w** and **r**	w**h**ere r**h**yme
b is almost always at the end of a word with the letter **m**	tom**b**
l (in the same syllable) comes between **a** and **k** **a** and **f** **a** and **v** **a** and **m** **o** and **k** before **d**	wa**l**k ca**l**f ha**l**ve ca**l**m yo**l**k wou**l**d
d comes before a consonant	e**d**ge
n usually follows an **m**	hym**n**
s comes before an **l**	ai**s**le
p is usually at the beginning of a word, often of Greek or Latin origin	**p**neumonia
t comes after an **s**	whis**t**le
c comes after an **s**	mus**c**le

The letter string 'ough'

The letter string **ough** can be used for a number of different sounds. Read the following words aloud to hear the difference.

enough	plough	bought	although

Words with the /ee/ sound spelled 'ei' and 'ie'

Normally, words that have a long **/ee/** sound are spelled **ie**.

shield	brief	yield

However, there are exceptions. For example:

seize	protein	weird

When the sound **/ee/** comes after the letter **c**, it is usually spelled **ei**.

ceiling	receive	perceive

The letters **ei** can also be pronounced as **/ay/**.

freight	weight	eight

Other exception words just need learning as there is no rule.

science	glacier

TRICKY SPELLINGS

PRACTICE

1. The following words have been spelled incorrectly: each word should contain a **silent letter**. Rewrite them correctly.

   a. colum   _____

   b. rombus   _____

   c. autum   _____

   d. iland   _____

   e. desent   _____

   f. casle   _____

2. Write the words below in the correct column according to the sound that their **ough letter string** makes, which should match the sound of the word at the top of the column.

enough	though	bough	ought

plough	thorough	fought	tough

trough	bought	dough	brought

rough	cough	slough

although	thought	borough

3. Circle the word that has been **spelled incorrectly** and write it (showing the correct spelling) on the line below each sentence.

   a. He was sacked for being deceitful so he didn't recieve a leaving present.

   _____

   b. The soldiers arrived weilding weapons but neither side had the strength to fight.

   _____

   c. Our neighbour's neice is arriving from Australia next week.

   _____

4. Group the words in the box below according to the **spelling rule** at the top of each column. Write your answers in the correct column.

   conscience   conceive   shriek   ancient   thief   receive

   siege   piece   seize   freight   deceit   caffeine

   protein   conceit   glacier   neighbour   fierce

Words with an **ie** spelling and an **/ee/** sound	Words with an **ei** spelling and an **/ee/** sound following a **c**	Words with an **ei** spelling and an **/ay/** sound	Exceptions

Answers

The answers are given below. They are referenced by page number and question number. The answers usually only include the information the children are expected to give. There may be some places where the answers vary or multiple answers are acceptable; these are marked as such. Note that in some places, answers will be varied and subjective from child to child, and a fair degree of marker discretion and interpretation is needed, particularly if children's understanding and skills have to be deduced from their answers.

Page	Q	Answers
7	1	a. We walked to the <u>shops</u> but took the <u>bus</u> back. b. Our <u>class</u> visited the <u>museum</u> yesterday.
	2	My <u>really</u> annoying sister is in trouble again.
	3	a. We <u>practised</u> our song until we <u>were</u> perfect. b. On Saturdays, Mia <u>goes</u> to the library and <u>chooses</u> a book.
	4	a. After a long day, I look forward to a hot soak in the bath. b. In the far distance, the sailors spotted a pirate ship.
	5	a. Answers will vary. Example: Dad switched off the light. (noun) b. Answers will vary. Example: Mum used a match to light the fire. (verb)
9	1	a. **it** refers to <u>the scooter</u>. b. **she** refers to <u>Megan</u>.
	2	That's not my coat, it's <u>yours</u>. <u>Mine</u> looks similar but I know <u>yours</u> has a missing button.
	3	<u>They</u> comforted <u>her</u> when <u>she</u> fell.
	4	a. Mum cooked Amelia and <u>me</u> a big breakfast. b. Flo and <u>I</u> had a picnic in the park. c. Dad and <u>I</u> worked in the garden all day.
	5	We had <u>a</u> last attempt at scoring <u>a</u> goal but <u>the</u> other team proved too strong for us.
	6	Example: <u>Those</u> children have dropped <u>that</u> litter so let's tell them to pick it up and put it in <u>these</u> bins.
	7	a. Archie passed the butter to <u>his</u> brother so he could butter <u>his</u> toast. b. <u>Our</u> grandparents like to travel to the seaside for <u>their</u> holidays. c. The boys picked up <u>their</u> books and put them back in <u>their</u> trays.
11	1	a. We <u>might</u> go swimming tonight. b. You <u>should</u> help your mum by tidying your room.
	2	Henry can speak two languages.
	3	Sadly, we think it is <u>unlikely</u> that our hockey team will win the final.
	4	We're definitely going to Scotland on holiday.
	5	Answers will vary. Examples: 1. If I won £100, I might go shopping in London or I may even use it to buy a new bike. 2. I definitely wouldn't share it with my little brother.
12	1	Mum is cooking spaghetti for our tea.
	2	Accept a suitable question, with an initial capital letter and final question mark, that would generate the answer, such as: How many legs do insects have?

Page	Q	Answers
13	3	<table><tr><th>Sentence</th><th>Statement</th><th>Question</th><th>Command</th><th>Exclamation</th></tr><tr><td>What time does the film start</td><td></td><td>✓</td><td></td><td></td></tr><tr><td>What an amazing display of flowers that is</td><td></td><td></td><td></td><td>✓</td></tr><tr><td>We are meeting Sam and Joe at the shops</td><td>✓</td><td></td><td></td><td></td></tr><tr><td>Mix all the ingredients together</td><td></td><td></td><td>✓</td><td></td></tr></table>
	4	Dan has a younger sister and an older brother, doesn't he?
	5	a. It doesn't have a verb. b. Answers may vary. Example: What a surprise it is to see you! What a surprise you had when the door flew open!
	6	Answers will vary. Examples: <table><tr><th>Sentence type</th><th>Sentence</th></tr><tr><td>exclamation</td><td>How lovely it was to see you last week!</td></tr><tr><td>question using a question tag</td><td>There are five days in a school week, aren't there?</td></tr><tr><td>statement</td><td>My favourite band is playing tonight.</td></tr><tr><td>command</td><td>Help me plant these seeds, please.</td></tr></table>

Page	Q	Answers
14	1	<table><tr><th>Sentence</th><th>Main clause</th><th>Subordinate clause</th></tr><tr><td>Even though she had eaten all her lunch, **Sophie was still hungry**.</td><td>✓</td><td></td></tr><tr><td>Bethan went to the dentist **after Mum picked her up from school**.</td><td></td><td>✓</td></tr><tr><td>**As you have been talking all morning**, you probably didn't hear my instructions.</td><td></td><td>✓</td></tr><tr><td>**It was clear that Maggie had practised her spellings** since she got every single one correct.</td><td>✓</td><td></td></tr></table>
15	2	It started to rain <u>so</u> we packed our waterproofs <u>and</u> wellies. I asked if we should bring umbrellas <u>but</u> Mum said no.
	3	a. Don't stand up <u>until</u> the train has stopped. b. Paula didn't know her 9-times tables <u>or</u> her 12-times tables.
	4	Answers will vary. Example: <u>Cara had travelled to many different countries</u> although she was only 11 years old.
	5	While she was helping Dad in the garden, Stella was stung by a wasp.
	6	Answers will vary. Examples: It's not a main clause because it doesn't make sense on its own. or It's not a main clause because it is dependent on 'Erin spent the day indoors' to make sense.
16	1	a. The head teacher <u>who visited from the neighbouring school</u> was impressed with our work. b. The boy <u>whose shoes had been found in lost property</u> was embarrassed. c. Otters are playful creatures <u>which live in clean rivers</u>. d. We saw layers of sedimentary rock <u>that were folded and twisted</u>.

ANSWERS

Page	Q	Answers
17	2	whose
	3	a. The investigation, <u>which</u> we started before break, took much longer than we thought. b. My uncle, <u>who</u> works for the local council, says pollution is a huge problem. c. Our neighbour, <u>whose</u> car was stolen last week, has had to get the bus to work. d. The day <u>when/that</u> I was born is famous for many other reasons!
	4	Our local restaurant, whose owners are from Spain, is closing next week.
	5	The boy to <u>whom</u> you were just talking is my cousin. His name is Sean <u>which</u> is Irish. The town <u>where</u> he lives is just outside Dublin.
18	1	a. We bought <u>some apples.</u> b. Dad baked <u>a cake</u>. c. <u>Our dog</u> is hungry. d. Please wash <u>the dishes</u>.
19	2	a. Finally, we arrived at <u>the quaint seaside town</u>. b. Out of the blue, <u>a mysterious stranger in a dark cloak</u> stepped in front of us. c. Mrs Wilkinson wore <u>a vibrant yellow hat with a bunch of red cherries on the side</u>. d. <u>The wolf with the sharp, white fangs</u> jumped off the rocks.
	3	She is <u>a determined, well-respected athlete</u> who has represented her country in international competitions.

Answers will vary. Examples:

Noun phrase	Expanded noun phrase
some sharks	some amazing sharks with sharp, blood-splattered teeth
a lot of people	a lot of loud people wearing fancy-dress outfits
the forest	the deep, dark forest's interior
two teachers	the two most annoying teachers

Page	Q	Answers
	5	Answers will vary. Examples: a. We saw some amazing sharks with sharp, blood-splattered teeth. b. There were a lot of loud people wearing fancy-dress outfits at the party. c. Into the deep, dark forest's interior we crept. d. They were the two most annoying teachers we had ever had the misfortune to meet!
21	1	a. I <u>brush</u> my teeth before I <u>go</u> to bed. b. After I <u>score</u> a goal, I <u>can't</u> stop smiling.
	2	Dad had just woken up when the phone began to ring.
	3	Our class <u>went</u> on a trip to the museum. We <u>saw</u> some Egyptian artefacts and <u>read</u> some hieroglyphic texts.
	4	a. We <u>are making</u> models of the Globe Theatre which we will display in the hall. b. Sian <u>is jumping</u> on the trampoline even though she has been told not to. c. Those dogs <u>are running</u> wild all over the park which is annoying. d. My sister <u>is crying</u> because Mum won't let her stay up late.
22	5	Have you seen my new pencil case?
	6	a. Alfie <u>was mumbling</u> that he didn't like sprouts or peas. b. We called Samir but he <u>was going</u> in the opposite direction. c. While we <u>were strolling</u> along the canal, we saw a shoal of fish and some ducks.
	7	My parents <u>have thought</u> about moving house. They <u>have viewed</u> a cottage in the countryside which I think they <u>have fallen</u> in love with.

Page	Q	Answers
23	8	In our class, there is one girl from Poland and there are two boys from India.
	9	Answers will vary. Accept sentences that use both simple past and past progressive tenses.

| 25 | 1 | |

Sentence	Active voice	Passive voice
Mum and Dad cheered me when I scored the winning goal.	✓	
The last piece of cake was eaten by my greedy little brother!		✓
Flo and Max found fossils in the rocks by the edge of the sea.	✓	
The messy art area was tidied by Scarlet.		✓

Page	Q	Answers
	2	a. Animal-loving <u>volunteers</u> care for the abandoned (pets). The abandoned pets were cared for by animal-loving volunteers. b. <u>Anya and Abigail</u> won the singing (competition). The singing competition was won by Anya and Abigail. c. <u>The head teacher</u> introduced the visiting (author). The visiting author was introduced by the head teacher.
	3	A local sports personality presented the trophy.
	4	Answers will vary. a. Accept a sentence written in the passive voice with an agent, using correct punctuation. b. Accept a sentence written in the passive voice without an agent, using correct punctuation.
26	1	It took Lucas ages to answer – the question being exceptionally hard – and everyone breathed a sigh of relief.
	2	a. My great-uncle (who seems pretty ancient) has just run a marathon. b. Chloe (determined and focused) summited the mountain in record time. c. The winning athletes (none of whom seemed out of breath) did a lap of honour. d. After an amazing birthday tea (pizza, coleslaw, ice cream and fruit), I blew out the candles on my birthday cake.
	3	Answers will vary. Accept suitable sentences, correctly punctuated with brackets, dashes and commas.
27	4	a. It's always cold in Edinburgh in the winter (though the Shetland Isles are colder still). b. Sam ordered a starter, main meal and a dessert (despite just having had a sandwich). c. We loved the play despite the main actor forgetting some of his lines (though only in the second act). d. Our teacher handed our tests back and I was thrilled with my mark (18 out of 20).
	5	Answers will vary. Examples: a. The doctor, always kind and caring, bandaged my arm expertly. b. Eating too much fried food (especially fatty meats) can lead to health problems. c. Our school library stocks many different genres – there is certainly something for everyone – but my favourite books are mysteries.
29	1	We came round the corner and faced the imposing door – the question on our lips was: should we open it?
	2	My friend Martha has a variety of qualities: she is kind, funny, thoughtful and cheerful.
	3	Dad's car ran out of petrol after ten miles; Mum couldn't believe he hadn't filled up before he left!
	4	In my rucksack, I have the following: equipment to boil water and a compass to show me directions.
	5	Answers will vary. Example: For our camping trip, we packed the following: waterproof coats; Wellington boots; woolly gloves and long, thick scarves.

ANSWERS

Page	Q	Answers
30	1	a. The pupil thinks that the teacher is improving in English. b. The teacher thinks that the pupil is improving in English.

31	2	Answers will vary. Examples:
		a. (i) The solicitor had to re-sign the will as a mistake had been made.
		   (ii)The Prime Minister had to resign from his position after the election.
		b. (i) The clouds re-formed in the sky so we knew rain wasn't far away.
		   (ii) Our school has been totally reformed following the appointment of a new head teacher.
		c. (i) As I had been interrupted, I had to re-count my money all over again.
		   (ii) I gave a great recount of my trip to France.

	3	a. The Lord Mayor is a <u>hard-working</u> man who rarely takes a holiday. b. My auntie Cath is a <u>silver-service</u> waitress in the best restaurant in town. c. Our school librarian was wearing a <u>light-blue</u> scarf.
	4	Answers will vary. Example: a. Please come to the table and eat Freya. b. Please come to the table and eat, Freya.
32	1	a. could not b. there is/has c. shall not d. they are e. would not have
	2	a. they had / they would b. I had / I would c. he is / he has
	3	There's no such thing as ghosts, we've been told.
33	4	See table below.

Word pairs/groups of words	Contracted form	Word pairs/groups of words	Contracted form
you are	you're	she has	she's
might not have	mightn't've	they are	they're
they had	they'd	Erin is	Erin's
can not	can't	should not have	shouldn't've
Stanley has	Stanley's	is not	isn't

Page	Q	Answers
34	1	The boys' jumpers were found in lost property.
35	2	See table below.

Phrase	Phrase with apostrophe
the books belonging to James	James's books
the wedding day of our parents	our parents' wedding day
the crown belonging to the princess	the princess's crown
the horses belonging to the princes	the princes' horses

Page	Q	Answers
35	3	a. The <u>men's</u> toilets were closed for refurbishment. b. My parents celebrated their anniversary on my <u>uncle's</u> boat. c. Our <u>class's</u> favourite subjects are art and geography. d. The <u>dresses'</u> collars are white and pointy and the pockets are a contrasting colour.
	4	Regular plural nouns: place the apostrophe after the final 's'. Irregular plural nouns: place the apostrophe after the final letter then add an 's'.

Page	Q	Answers
36	1	"How unbelievable that you are wearing the same dress as me!" exclaimed Mia.
37	2	"It's time to get in the car," said Dad. "Otherwise, we'll never get there." I ran down the stairs, grabbed my bag and jumped into the car. Dad started the engine. "Mum's going to make us late if she doesn't come soon," he grumbled. Luckily, at that moment, Mum came out of the house, locked the door and got into the car. "Have you turned off the television?" asked Dad. "Oh no!" exclaimed Mum. "I'm pretty sure I haven't."
	3	a. "I will announce the winner after lunch," said the judge. or The judge said, "I will announce the winner after lunch." b. Mum said, "If you don't tidy your bedroom, you can't go to the park." or "If you don't tidy your bedroom, you can't go to the park," said Mum. c. "I am very pleased with the work you have done in the garden," said Dad. or Dad said, "I am very pleased with the work you have done in the garden."
	4	a. The first inverted commas are double and the second are single. b. The question mark is outside the final inverted commas.
39	1	<u>un</u>believable; <u>in</u>destructible; <u>mis</u>inform; <u>ir</u>responsible; <u>de</u>compose; <u>il</u>logical
	2	Answers will vary. Examples: interrupt, disrupt, interruption, disruption
	3	(see table below)
	4	Answers will vary. Examples: a. recover: It took a long time for my grandpa to recover from his fall. b. re-cover: Mum decided to re-cover the armchair with a new fabric. c. represent: It is important to behave well on trips as we represent the school. d. re-present: The judge had to re-present the trophy as some of the team had been missing.

Words	Prefix meaning
subway	under/below
autobiography	self
bisect	two
monotone	one
universal	all

ANSWERS

Page	Q	Answers
41	1	Answers will vary: **Word / Word + suffix / Sentence** differ / difference / I noticed a big difference in my fitness after I started training. transfer / transferring / Mum is transferring some money to Dad's account. infer / inferred / The author inferred that the hero would return in the next book.
	2	**Nouns / Adjectives** consideration / considerate adoration / adorable terror / terrible resident / residential dependant/dependency / dependable/dependent application / applicable preference / preferable/preferred vacation/vacancy / vacant correspondent / corresponding
43	1	walk slowly
	2	calm
	3	chivalrous and courteous
	4	Answers will vary. Example: Mr Harris, who is <u>diligent</u>, <u>honest</u> and <u>considerate</u>, received a round of applause from the audience as he collected his award.
	5	a. <u>mis</u>inform b. <u>im</u>practical c. <u>in</u>credible d. <u>il</u>logical
44	1	a. Shila hasn't got any homework tonight. or Shila has not got any homework tonight. b. Give those books to me.
45	2	were
	3	I am delighted to welcome our esteemed guest, Mr Joseph Bloggs. → Formal speech It ain't half good to see you, Joe. → Informal speech Was you surprised to see Joe here? → No subject-verb agreement Here he is – welcome to the one and only Joseph Bloggs! → Non-Standard English
	4	We <u>were</u> at the cinema with our friends.
	5	We haven't seen our cousins for about a year.

Page	Q	Answers
46	1	a. Mike <u>towed</u> / toad the boat to the coast. b. The Three Wise Men arrived <u>bearing</u> / baring gifts. c. Mum's favourite cereal / <u>serial</u> is on TV tonight. d. The bridegroom walked down the <u>aisle</u> / isle with his bride.
	2	a. guessed b. wail c. affected d. principal
47	3	Answers will vary.
	4	advice / advise accept / except wary / weary access / excess

Answers may vary.

Greek prefix	Meaning	English word
agros	cultivated land	agriculture
gigas	enormous	gigantic
autos	self	automatic/autobiography/autograph
tele	far off	telescope/television

(Page 48, Q1)

2 sound

Q3:

tri — 3
hex — 6
mono — 1
deca — 10

4
a. finite   finish   infinity   final   (fine)
b. transport   transfer   (tranquil)   transit   transatlantic

Answers will vary.

Latin	Definition	English word
cent	hundred	centenary
alter	change	alternative
spectare	watch	spectacle
audire	hear	audition

(Page 49, Q5)

6
a. Answers may vary. Examples: visible, invisible, vista, vision, visual
b. see

ANSWERS

Page	Q	Answers
52	1	a. column b. rhombus c. autumn d. island e. descent f. castle
	2	(see tables below)

rough	cough	slough
enough tough	trough	plough bough

although	thought	borough
though dough	ought fought bought brought	thorough

Page	Q	Answers
53	3	a. He was sacked for being deceitful so he didn't (recieve) a leaving present. receive b. The soldiers arrived (weilding) weapons but neither side had the strength to fight. wielding c. Our neighbour's (neice) is arriving from Australia next week. niece
	4	(see table below)

Words with an **ie** spelling and an **/ee/** sound	Words with an **ei** spelling and an **/ee/** sound following a **c**	Words with an **ei** spelling and an **/ay/** sound	Exceptions
shriek thief piece siege	conceive receive deceit conceit	freight neighbour	seize protein caffeine ancient conscience glacier fierce

Notes

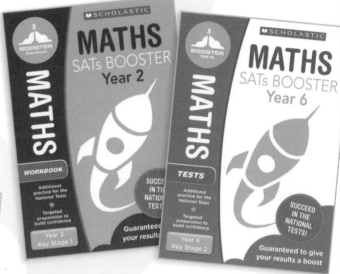

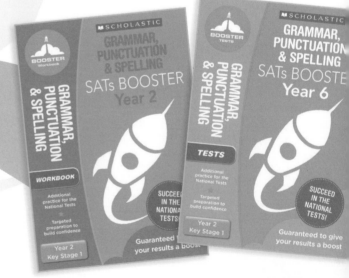